Nature's Peace

A Celebration of
Scotland's Watershed

Climb the mountains and get their good tidings.
Nature's peace will flow into you as sunshine
flows into trees. The winds will blow their
freshness into you, and the storms their energy,
while cares will drop off like autumn leaves.
JOHN MUIR

Nature's Peace

A Celebration of
Scotland's Watershed

PETER WRIGHT

Luath Press Limited

EDINBURGH

www.luath.co.uk

First published 2013

ISBN: 978-1-908373-83-0

The paper used in this book is recyclable.
It is made from low chlorine pulps produced
in a low energy, low emissions manner
from renewable forests.

The publishers acknowledge the support of

ALBA | CHRUTHACHAIL

towards the publication of this volume.

Printed and bound by
Bell & Bain Ltd., Glasgow

Map by Jim Lewis

Typeset in 11 point Quadraat
by 3btype.com

Dedication

Nature's Peace is dedicated to all those who voluntarily take the time and the trouble to inspire a love of Nature's wild places in those around them, especially in young people. Their generous influence is a beacon of goodness, which touches many lives, and enriches the human spirit.

Contents

Foreword

The immense fund of inspiration about the Natural World that we can draw upon from the writings of John Muir is even more cogent today than it was when he first committed his thoughts and feelings to paper over a hundred years ago. That *Nature's Peace*, the title of this book, should be selected from one of his most popular quotes, is fitting indeed, as we prepare to mark the centenary of his death and reflect on his legacy. It gives me particular pleasure to provide a brief introduction to a book that will surely be appreciated and enjoyed by many. Peter Wright has created a landmark in the ever growing library of books about the landscapes of Scotland.

Although the concept of the Watershed, the backbone of Scotland, may be a very simple one, the landscapes of this geographic feature demonstrate a complex mix of widely differing types of terrain, and the rich habitats that they support. The evident wildness that binds all this together gives it a unique distinction, one that is noteworthy and invites celebration. People play an essential part in all of this, with a pride in their particular parts of the Watershed, and for those who visit from elsewhere, there is unlimited fulfilment and potential challenge.

The collection of pictures in *Nature's Peace* take us on an evocative journey, spurred on by the evident talents of the many photographers who have contributed so generously to this fine book. Each has captured something of what they both saw and felt about the many different locations on this special journey, and given us something to enjoy. Together, they have provided the means to appreciate the landform of Scotland in a new way.

So, it is my hope that you will find something enriching for both mind and spirit within the pages of *Nature's Peace*, that you will discover a new dimension to the landscapes of Scotland, and capture for yourself a good measure of Muir's love of wild places. I also hope that this book inspires you to take your own journey into the wild and think about how you can 'do something for wildness and make the mountains glad'.

Stuart Brooks
CHIEF EXECUTIVE, JOHN MUIR TRUST

Acknowledgements

Many motivated and generous people have contributed to *Nature's Peace*, and in a variety of different ways.

I am especially grateful to Alex Wood for the professionalism, attention to detail and practical advice which he so freely gave in the editing and proofreading that he carried out. To Liz Lefroy for her tact and skill in helping focus my poetic effort. To the following people who have used their photographic skills and talents to such good effect, and captured so many landscapes and moments – indeed the very essence of *Nature's Peace*: Keith Brame, David Lintern, Nancy Chinnery, John Thomas, Ruth Longmuir, Hannah Longmuir, Malcolm Wylie, Gavin Crosby, Kerry Muirhead, Nick Bramhall, Chris Townsend, Fraser McAlistair, Peter Woolverton, Anna Woolverton, David MacFarlane, Katrina Martin, Mary Bates, Marie Lainton, Kirsty Bloom, Colin Meek, Nick McLaren, Norrie Russel, Colin Gregory, Fiona Isbister, NTS Library, Mike Pennington, Calum Toogood, Frank Hay, Kenneth Wright, James Wright, Mike Watson, Jen Trendall, Richard Kermode, Alan Bowie, James Macpherson, Richard King, Nigel Brown, Larry Foster, Jim Shedden, Rob Beaumont, Frank Brown, Richard Webb, Chris Dyer, John Tulloch, Hayley Warriner, Calum Togood, Kathryn Goodenough, Ewan Lyons, Andy Hunter, John Ferguson, Stephen Middlemiss, Andy Wilby and Jim deBank.

Peter Wright

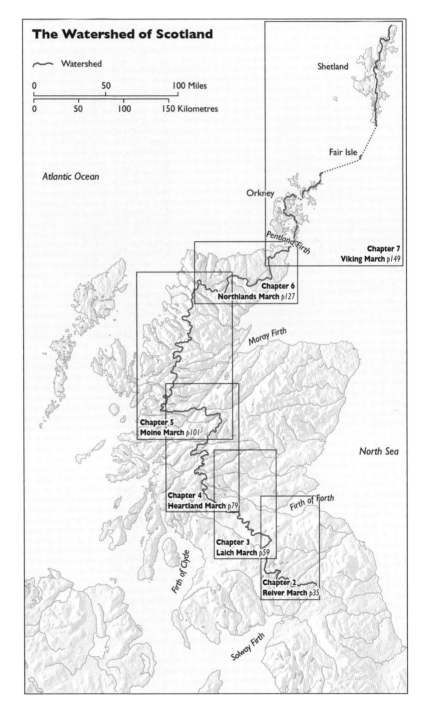

The Watershed of Scotland

Watershed

| 0 | 50 | 100 Miles |
| 0 | 50 | 100 | 150 Kilometres |

Shetland

Atlantic Ocean

Fair Isle

Orkney

Pentland Firth

Chapter 7
Viking March p149

Chapter 6
Northlands March p127

Moray Firth

Chapter 5
Moine March p101

North Sea

Chapter 4
Heartland March p79

Firth of Forth

Chapter 3
Laich March p59

Firth of Clyde

Chapter 2
Reiver March p35

Solway Firth

Great Glen Sunset

The wonder of sunset upon
the Great Glen to Loch Ness,
from Creag nan Gobhar.
Kirsty Bloom, Great Glen Hostel
NN315985

Nature's Peace

Come, come away from the crowd,
take unhurried time,
leave the familiar order of things
and dare.

Discover Nature's high places,
and go beyond the mundane to push yourself.
Tread lightly upon this fine green ribbon in the landscape
to find more of your spirit,
in all the possibilities
of this promising engagement
with wildness.

PETER WRIGHT

Carrifran Fencewalkers

Fence-walkers pause on their patrol round the high rim of Carrifran Wildwood, Borders Forest Trust.

John Thomas, John Muir Trust

NT159138

Chapter One

Welcome to the Watershed – *Our Ribbon of Wildness*

Do something for wildness and make the mountains glad. JOHN MUIR

Within the pages of *Nature's Peace*, you are invited to imagine yourself taking an immense journey along the entire length of Scotland, on the very spine of the country. The many photographs will give you a tantalising flavour of just some of the magnificent landscapes to be experienced along the way, by hill, mountain, rock, moor and forest. These images may evoke memories of other journeys and from each of these, may also develop a very personal growing love of our wilder landscapes. They may re-kindle your awareness of places not yet visited, but very much on your *wish list*. While for the walker they will stimulate a fond recollection of many fine days out on the hill. In *Nature's Peace*, there is an entirely novel visual experience of a vast swathe of much of Scotland's best countryside, on an original route from the border with England all the way to Unst in Shetland, by way of Duncansby Head in Caithness. It proudly connects, then presents, and enthusiastically celebrates a large slice of Scotland as you have never quite seen it before.

The recognition and enjoyment of the great Watershed of

Stacks of Duncansby
Stacks of Duncansby stand like a guard of honour to mark the inspiring approach to Duncansby Head.
Colin Gregory,
Thurso Camera Club
ND397715

Blackwater Reservoir

Light on water and range
beyond range – Blackwater
Reservoir and Glencoe from
Sron Leachd a Chaorainn.

Peter Wright
NN419629

Ben Alisky and Morven
Morven framed by the Watershed's twin tops of Ben Alisky and Beinn Glas-choire.
Colin Gregory,
Thurso Camera Club
ND039387

Scotland offers an opportunity to do something for Scotland, her people and her visitors, of almost unrivalled integrity. It most certainly provides an opportunity to '*do something for wildness*', as Muir so eloquently invites. As an addition to the gazetteer of Scotland, it creates a radical dimension to how we see and appreciate the landform of this country. For those who love all that Nature has bestowed, and are tuned in to that eternal heartbeat, there is an eco-spiritual enrichment in these special landscapes.

This golden opportunity has a head start, for it already binds a large number of designated and protected sites, and every single national environmental organisation has an active presence. Many local conservation groups have a direct interest in their local landscapes which form an integral part of it. It is *Scotland United* – *by Nature*, by wildness.

Those who travel around Scotland and appreciate the great landscapes that this country has to offer will in all likelihood have crossed and re-crossed the Watershed on countless occasions, perhaps without even being aware of it. Many writers have drawn attention to that special moment when the traveller will *cross the Watershed*, almost as a right of passage, perhaps to some other exciting destination elsewhere.

South from Culter Fell
Lone walker and boot-marks
in the snow leading south from
Culter Fell to Gathersnow Hill
and Hillshaw Head.
Anna Woolverton
NT052291

How does this all link together to form the great Watershed of Scotland; indeed, what is this apparently novel geographic feature which has mysteriously appeared? In the United Kingdom the picture is paradoxically sketchy, while north of the border, there are but two historical references, by Francis H. Groome in 1884 and then in the Collins Survey Atlas of Scotland of 1912 – both of which allude to the geographic Watershed. Yet, what we have is an intriguingly simple divide between, on the one hand the Atlantic Ocean and those bodies of water that are directly connected to it, such as the Solway Firth, the Irish Sea and The Minch, while to the east there is just the North Sea.

A small number of intrepid people have now walked and indeed run the Watershed in whole or in part. The first to walk the fully defined geographic Watershed was Malcolm Wylie. Dave Hewitt accomplished an impressive continuous walk along much of the Watershed some years earlier, with a Northern terminus at Cape Wrath – top left-hand corner. The author undertook his backpack Watershed trek in stages in 2005, and in 2012, Colin Meek completed an incredible Watershed run. Chris Townsend will be the most recent with his venture in summer 2013. Others have contributed to this walking genre by undertaking their own version or particular part of it.

This very brief dip into the Watershed on-foot phenomenon is surely beginning to provide a graphic explanation of just what this key landscape feature is. To round it off, however, the concept is indeed a simple one, and a number of people have remarked that it is strange that something so simple has not been more widely promoted and celebrated much sooner.

So the classic description goes as follows: '*Imagine that you are a*

Eskdalemuir

The enticing upper-Eskdale, with a Watershed source rising to the left of this landscape.
Nancy Chinnery,
Eskdalemuir Community Hub
NY243990

raindrop about to land on Scotland, well your destiny dear raindrop is that when you do touch-down, you will start another journey by bog, burn and river. Finally, you will empty into either the Atlantic Ocean or the North Sea, and which it is to be will depend upon which side of the spine of the country – the Watershed, or water divide – you have first landed'.

The most detailed definition and description of the Watershed of Scotland has been given in the author's own *Ribbon of Wildness – Discovering the Watershed of Scotland* published by Luath Press in

Black Law Wind farm
Desirable or destructive – the dilemma of turbines on the Watershed, and Black Law.
Peter Wright
NS910550

2010. The Royal Scottish Geographical Society in response to this, in 2011, described the Watershed as '*this hitherto largely unknown geographic feature*'. Whilst *The Scotsman* had this to say: '*No other journey can give so sublime a sense of unity, a feeling of how the Nation's various landscapes link together to form a coherent whole*'. Clearly public awareness is changing year on year, and there can be no more fitting events than the Year of Natural Scotland in 2013 and John Muir Centenary during 2014 to ensure that the Watershed of

Ben Alder

Snow and mist remnants on the hill – Ben Alder from Sgor Gaibhre, over Beinn a Chumhainn.

Richard Kermode
NN469718

Scotland is more widely and popularly appreciated – simply for what it is.

This does of course beg the question as to why the Watershed should be of such growing importance, and from this, why should it be valued in a way that has not been the case hitherto?

We have of course, a bit of catching up to do with other countries and continents, where the key place and function of the Watershed in their respective landforms is fully appreciated, celebrated even. We have the growing range of hard copy and online accounts of the on foot journeys along all or part of the Watershed, and these are nothing if not inspiring. Indeed, the common thread is that the *route* was created not by mankind; not in any way for our convenience, but solely by the hand of Nature. There are a growing body of people who are fascinated by the immensity of the forces, timescales, events, and processes that have given us this Watershed, and put it where it is. It is certainly largely unchanged in location, since the end of the last Ice Age, while many parts of it extend much further back into geo-glacial time. True, its surface and habitat character have changed greatly over these thousands and millions of years, but location and where water starts its further journey by bog, via burn and river, is largely unaltered.

This alone, however, will not suffice as a reason for conservation; the historical dimension is only a part of the story. Much has rightly been done of late to identify, describe and give critical importance to wild land, and to mark out the value of wildness in our landscapes. There will be those who argue that *wild land* and *wildness* may not necessarily be one and the same thing, and they may produce factors which set them apart. The processes and methods of defining wild-land may be emerging as a more exact science, but the areas thus defined are sadly shrinking – both on account of increasing precision in the criteria being used and of the inexorable encroachment into these very areas, by man-made structures. Most are naturally far from the main centres of population, and herein lies both a dilemma and a challenge. These areas are unquestionably worth greater protection, but their very remoteness, often at the extremity or boundary of both estate and local authority, serve to

Blar nam Faoileag Sunset
Winter sunset catching an extensive area of Flows, from above Blar nam Faoileag, to Morven.
Norrie Russel, RSPB Forsinard
ND131453

**After the Snow Flurry –
Borders Hills**
Texture of light catching snow
covered tussocks, under a
heavy sky in the Border Hills.
Peter Wright
NT558019

Below
Bodesbeck Law
Lochan on the edge of the deep
steep crags on Black Hope to
the inviting Bodesbeck Law,
with Mirk Side on the left.
Anna Woolverton
NT169104

marginalise their priority. They are however something well worth arguing for.

The meaning of the relative concept of *wildness* may have changed subtly since Muir's day, but in a way that it is argued, demands a more inclusive approach; it surely implies something with immense, almost unlimited potential – for people. It is something which we

can all engage with, something which invites participation; something from which we can all draw strength and renewal.

Wildness and weather are certainly closely related. Any notion that the Watershed bathes in never-ending sunshine, no matter how appealing all of the pictures in this book are, would be misleading. To illustrate this point, the author cites his own experience throughout much of his trek in 2005. Of the 64 days of walking, the visibility was poor for around one third of the time, and on just two of these days the weather was also marred by torrential rain and wind. Not a bad record in fact. But it should be remembered that with an average elevation of some 470m, parts of it are inevitably shrouded in mist, but that is one of the tantalising qualities of the outdoor experience – unpredictability.

It would indeed be intriguing to be able to welcome John Muir back to the land of his birth, and to see what he would make of it today. The John Muir Trust is the worthy and effective custodian of his legacy. The very least that we can do is to actively support this organisation in all that it does. We can be sure that there is

Lochcraig Head
Evidence of a severe cold-spell with ice-encrusted post on Lochcraig Head.
Keith Brame
NT167176

Below
White Hill Cloud Inversion
Island of woodland in a cloud inversion east of White Hill above Dolphinton.
Peter Wright
NT089469

much in both the theme and landscape character described here in
Nature's Peace that Muir would have commented upon had it been
possible, and we can only speculate on what he might have said
to us. It would not be unreasonable therefore to imagine a virtual
visit, and to posit his verdict on the Watershed at least, towards
the end of this book.

As a means of making the Watershed a bit more comprehensible
– well over 1,100km of indirect meander running the length
of mainland Scotland, as well as its continuation through the
Northern Isles, is a long route by any standards, so the author
has broken it down into six more manageable sections and called
them *Marches* – this being the traditional word for a boundary.

RIEVER MARCH comes first. It runs from Peel Fell on the
border with England, to the
Southern Uplands Fault line, just
south of Biggar.

LAICH or low **MARCH** comes
next, traversing the central belt,
as far as Guilan on the Highland
Boundary Fault, near the south
eastern corner of Loch Lomond.

Sgurr nan Ceannaichean
Signs of a sloping strata and streaks of water-scoured gullies on Sgurr nan Ceannaichean, from the west.
Nigel Brown, Geograph protocol
NH086480

Below
Glenbeg Bothy
Snowline contrast of winter colours around Glenbeg Bothy towards Meall Feith na Slataich end of Seana Bhraigh.
James Macpherson,
Mountain Bothies Association
NH313835

This is followed by the **HEARTLAND MARCH** which takes the route to the Great Glen Fault, at Laggan, north east of Loch Lochy.

The longest of these Marches is **MOINE** which carries the Watershed through the west and north-west Highlands to Ben Hee, above Loch Shin.

The **NORTHLANDS MARCH** spans the entire Flow Country

Sail Garbh
Among the rocky loop in the
north-west, from Sail Garbh
to Meall a Chleirich and Carn
Deerg beyond.
Nick McLaren
NC406347

Unst and Yell

Inviting blue sea and sky with white sand across Bluemull Sound to Unst.

NTS photo library
HP549010

in Sutherland and Caithness, to its conclusion on mainland Scotland, at Duncansby Head.

The place of the Orkney and Shetland Islands in the story of defining the Watershed in geographic terms is covered in some detail in *Ribbon of Wildness*, so it is entirely logical to bring these archipelagos into this volume. This new part to the route can be plotted from South Ronaldsay overlooking the Pentland Firth, through mainland Orkney and some of the North Isles, and from there across to remote Fair Isle. The final destination is at Muckle Flugga on Unst in Shetland, where the beam of light from the lighthouse sweeps across the Norwegian Sea. There, Atlantic Ocean and North Sea have become one. This section is called the VIKING MARCH.

As a geographic and landscape feature of such magnitude, which demonstrates largely continuous wildness and can indeed, be seen as an artery of Nature, the Watershed as a whole has a unique character. This begs a clear question: how can the Watershed be used to provide a single Scotland-long environmental focus? People will be affected by it in a variety of different ways, but for many, it has all the promise of offering an eco-spiritual experience. A longer term vision for the Watershed is offered as both a mark and as a fitting legacy for the John Muir Centenary. Within these pages, you will find more of the evidence for this, the photographs telling a beguiling and compelling story.

Do enjoy this great journey on which you are embarking within these pages. If you bring with you a measure of good humour, curiosity and a love of wildness, you will most certainly not be disappointed.

**Bodesbeck Law from
Swatte Fell**

Delights of the magical Moffat
Hills with Bodesbeck Fell,
from Black Craig.

Peter Wooverton

HT118113

Opposite

**Peel Fell from
Deadwater Moor**

The author gesturing from
Deadwater Moor tarn towards
Peel Fell, the southern terminus
and start of this epic.

Colin Meek

NY630976

Chapter Two

The Reiver March – *Through the Southern Uplands*

Take a course in good water and air;
and in the eternal youth of Nature
you may renew your own.
Go quietly, alone;
no harm will befall you. JOHN MUIR

This, the Reiver March, is the curtain-raiser, the introduction to a singularly spectacular visual journey through a vast swathe of the Scottish landscape. It sets the scene for this radical new means of appreciation, of understanding more, of the landform, centred so dramatically upon the spine of the country.

Peel Fell, where it all starts, is at a cross roads between the Watershed of the entire United Kingdom, and the frontier between England and Scotland. The Watershed has long been where it is – since at least the end of the last Ice Age, a fact which puts our brief place in the landscape of things into perspective.

Peel Fell

Texture and light on
winter's-end vegetation under
a heavy sky – Peel Fell from
Hartshorn Pike.
Gavin Crosby
NY625997

St Mary's Loch From Herman Law

Enchanting hills and water, with Tibbie Shiel's between Lochs of the Lowes and St Mary's, from Herman Law.

Kerry Muirhead, Ettrick and Yarrow Valleys

NT213157

Moss Law and Holms Nick

Inviting autumn light spread
across the shoulder of Moss
Law and Hillshaw Head,
from Woodycleuch Dod.
Peter Wright
NT026296

Peel Fell Landscape
Views south over Kielder
Forest and Water to the
Lakeland Fells are briefly lost,
but Peel Fell has promise.
Gavin Crosby
NY625997

Standing on the summit of Peel Fell, there is a powerful sense of place, of major familiar landmarks, that set this hill in a much wider context. It is worth taking the time to marvel. The two major English landmarks are The Cheviot to the east, and hence in the North East of England, whilst to the south of this vantage point, the distinctive profile of the Lakeland Fells catches the eye. Continuing the panorama in a clockwise direction, the Solway Firth weaves a silver widening way towards the Irish Sea, with Criffel and the Galloway coast as pointers. To the west lies the great expanse of the forests, including Craik and Eskdalemuir. That great river, the Tweed and its vast basin fed by Teviot, Ettrick, Yarrow and a multitude of other burns, fills the north of this great vista, with the Lammermuir Hills beyond.

The cairn on the summit of Peel Fell is but a modest heap of stones, which perhaps underplays its new-found place upon the Watershed. But it abounds in habitat status, its surrounding moors and bogs protected by being both a Special Area of Conservation (SAC) and a Site of Special Scientific Interest (SSSI).

This designation is neither random nor out of place with the rest of the Watershed, for there follow a formidable roll call of such important and protected sites, with almost 90 covering six of the most significant legal habitat designations on the mainland, and a further array of sites in the Northern Isles of Orkney and Shetland.

History is never far below the surface here. Roman soldiers, Norman knights, Border Reivers, mail coachmen, railway engineers and solitary shepherds have all left their subtle marks. While the line of the Watershed holds to the high ground, and much of this human activity will have been at its crossings, the events are commemorated in book and ballad. Some are relived as a vibrant community's sense of itself, with for example, the Mosspaul Ride-out, part of the Hawick Common Riding each June, in which horse, rider, banner and song proclaim an ancient tradition – a popular part of that community's calendar.

The route being followed lies in the hills which are generally known as the Southern Uplands. Much of it is on or within the boundary of the Scottish Borders, a major part of it bounds with

Ettrick Pen From Bloodhope Head

The lichened cairn is a fine marker for Bloodhope Head with its view to Ettrick Pen, or The Pen of Eskdalemuir.

Kerry Muirhead, Ettrick and Yarrow Valleys

NT226097

Loch Skeen Outflow

Four resolute figures cross a frozen landscape at the outfall to Loch Skeen viewed from Watch Knowe.

Keith Brame
NT176159

Below

Carrifran Wildwood Team

Borders Forest Trust's inspirational Carrifran Wildwood aims to re-establish a woodland habitat of six millennia ago.

John Thomas, John Muir Trust
NT151132

Dumfries and Galloway, and the final part with South Lanarkshire.

Throughout the Reiver March, the River Tweed, its catchment and all of its headwaters fall away to the right, making their mossy genesis here on the Watershed; this is all North Sea bound. To the left, the Solway Firth beckons for Liddel, Esk, Moffat, and Annan waters, and from Clyde Law, the great river of the same name takes over the drainage systems. Each of these river valleys have settlements of ancient pedigree, which grew from the power and sustenance which the pure water provided for industry and living.

Land use can only be viewed over long periods of time,

Fig. 2.

Clyde Law Windfarm

The appealing beauty of hilltop
sun and snow is marred by
the industrialisation of this
landscape on Clyde Law.
David Lintern
NT027170

**Glencotho from
Gathersnow Hill**

Great rewards in the last of the
winter snow across hill after hill
at Holm Nick and Glencotho
from Gathersnow Hill.

Anna Woolverton
NT058257

whether in its economic, social or habitat impact. Much of the
area around the western part of this March was part of the ancient
Royal Forest of Ettrick, but all changed in the 16th century
when James V turned it into a vast sheep run. A new way of life
then emerged, what we would now call 'hill sheep farming'.
This brought prosperity to some, and created the particular
skills of shepherding. The impact which this new land-use
had on these hills was considerable; habitats were greatly
altered and wildlife had to adapt.

In the second half of the 20th century, a further major change
occurred – the forestry industry arrived. A long slow decline in
the sheep farming community and way of life set in, a new tree-
clad landscape form became the norm. Over these centuries, the
key driver has been economic; quite simply, will it be profitable?

**Peel Fell Towards
The Solway**

A louring sky fails to conceal
the possibility of distant views
from Peel Fell into the North-
West of England.

Gavin Crosby
NY625997

Below

**Hartshorn Pike from
Peel Fell**

The detail and texture of lichen
and moss on haunches of rock
enrich the view from Peel Fell
to Hartshorn Pike.

Gavin Crosby
NY625997

Greatmoor Hill from Cauldcleuch Head

Contrast of forest on northern slopes up to the fenceline, with the open folds of Greatmoor Hill from Caulcleuch Head.

Peter Wright
NT457004

While to this have now been added government policy, some environmental considerations and tax advantage, usually for those with no direct local interest. Although it will be interesting to see how this all works out for these uplands and the people living in them, over the next 50 or a hundred years, it is strongly argued that for all of the reasons presented in *Ribbon of Wildness*, in these pages, and by growing popular consent, the Watershed merits particular effort. It is an environmental gem which should be polished, not tarnished.

The author is concerned here primarily with what he has come to refer to as the ribbon of wildness, and with many of the factors that contribute to or potentially detract from its landscape quality. A growing concern is the issue of wind farms, and their impact – current or potential, on this, the higher ground. The Watershed is, in a sense, a very long ridge and in many parts it is prominent visually, it is one of the key, if hitherto under-sung geographic features, which should place it much higher in the conservation stakes. The Reiver March has alas not escaped the incursion of ill-conceived wind farms, and at the time of writing, more of these inappropriate erections are proposed. This is a theme which will crop up again along the way, but those local people living in and about these particular hills deserve both wider support and encouragement in their endeavour to oppose such plans.

In the bigger picture, the economics of many wind farms whether built or advocated, simply do not stack up. Were it not for the generous renewables subsidies, for which we all pay, the entire industry would be unsound. The John Muir Trust and others have done much to argue this case, and we all benefit from the time, skill, and clear-thinking which they continue to invest in this. The main beneficiaries of wind farms are the land owners, and their objective could only regard as a *quick buck*. While local communities are often offered a sop to buy their grateful appreciation: in no way does this merit the environmental blight thus created. So how can the needs of legitimate local interests be fairly sustained, against the might of National policy and incentive?

Two national forms of land designation and protection are present here at four sites on the Reiver March, with both Sites of Special Scientific Interest (SSSI) and Special Area of Conservation

Langtae Hill to Cauldcleuch Head

Afternoon light catches moor grasses and early bog cotton along the rim of Langtae Sike to Cauldcleuch Head.

Peter Wright
NT441002

Blue Cairn Hill to Bloodhope Head
A final forest-ride from Bluecairn Hill creates a sense of anticipation of more open terrain following Bloodhope Head.
Kerry Muirhead
NT235090

(SAC). Three key environmental organisations have an active presence, with the National Trust for Scotland (NTS) owning one site, The Borders Forest Trust owning two sites, on which it has worked in partnership with the John Muir Trust (JMT). Three very different kinds of terrain are present in the 140 km which the Reiver March covers.

Forest Hills

Leaving the moors and peat hags of Peel Fell behind, and moving north on this, the great Watershed of Scotland, first by Hartshorn Pike, the sense of anticipation is palpable. The mind is crowded with questions. How well has this traveller prepared for the journey; for planning, equipment, fitness, and navigation skills are all going to be tested to the full? What unforeseen events or challenges will be met along the way? What particular demands will the weather bring? Will this journey along the very backbone of the country realise all the promise of fine views, and dramatic panoramas?

More immediately though, how can this vast forest be traversed safely? The sultry green cloak of Wauchope, Craik and Eskdalemuir Forests creep up on either side of the Watershed

for much of the first 60km of this March, with only a few areas of open moor and hill, to relieve the dark shadows. For these are dense commercial forests, planted ostensibly to reduce the National dependence on imported timber. We remain a net importer, so these and other commercial forests are here to stay, but modest and much welcome change is on the way, with a softer environmental approach to restocking, or second generation planting. In theory, the higher ground and the water courses will be left clear, with scope for much greater habitat diversity and all of the wildlife benefits which this will bring. It remains to be seen however, just how rigidly this promised new regime will be implemented.

Although this may seem to be a rather gloomy and certainly cautious view, one great positive has emerged, and this is that the Watershed has remained intact, it has survived as a narrow forest ride, with the remains of a fence line running up the middle of it. This is indeed narrow in places, perhaps not much more than 20m in width, but in other locations it is more substantial. It remains therefore, as an unploughed, unplanted tract of rather rank but more or less intact vegetation that predates the coming of the trees on either side of it. It is therefore of immense value, as it will act as a seedbed for regeneration on the broader expanse which should be left clear in the re-stocking plans. Over time, Nature will hopefully reclaim her own and the biodiversity will be more firmly

Ettrick Valley
Purple heather-clad hills line the upper Ettrick Valley as it wends towards its Watershed source.
Frank Brown,
Ettrick and Yarrow Valleys
NT311194

**Croft Head from
Capel Fell**

Capel Fell affords fine views
over steep scree-girt slopes to
Croft Head and overlooking
Southern Upland Way.

Peter Wooverton

NT163069

established. This will attract a much greater range of plant, bird
and animal life than could ever have survived in the commercial
forest. One of the campaigns that needs to be waged in this, the
Forest Hills section of the Reiver March, is that all the promise
of the benefits from restocking should in fact be realised. This
will affect both the practices of the Forestry Commission and the
private foresters alike.

The areas of open hill and moor come as a fine opportunity to
walk more easily on the shorter grazed vegetation, and to take in
the views of the surrounding uplands. They afford great vistas to
distant features and horizons. It is a delight to pause in order to
identify distinctive outcrops like the Eildon Hills to the north and
admire the wide expanse of the Tweed Valley basin. The tangible
visual link with the North-West of England and towards the Irish
Sea to the south, is immensely appealing, and helps to describe
our place here in the wider landform of Scotland. This intense
sense of place in the much greater physical geography of the
country will undoubtedly be a recurring theme, one which will
invite the traveller to pause frequently, on this epic journey.

Apart from a small lochan on the summit of Hartshorn Pike,
there is only one other loch in this the Forest Hills section.

Moodlaw Loch, between Archie Hill and Black Knowe had the unusual distinction of being the meeting point of three counties; Dumfriesshire, Roxburghshire and Selkirkshire. With no apparent inlet or outlet, it is something of a conundrum. However it provides a delightful surprise in the forest, with dancing reflected light, and a real contrast with the surrounding forest.

Moffat Hills

As the Watershed climbs out of the forest by Blue Cairn Hill to Bloodhope Head, there is a real sense of anticipation, as one habitat is rapidly replaced by another. That 200m ascent from forest to fell, takes the route into a new world. The next 60km will be marked by three great sweeps round the headwaters of Ettrick, Moffat and Tweed waters, in an immense s-shaped gesture.

Much of the upper Ettrick valley is now given over to forestry, but apart from one small section at Glendearg Steps, all of the tops are clear and free of these trees. The habitats here are rich and varied, the views rewarding, and the terrain is firm. Navigation is not hard, with a fence or dyke to follow much of the way – this is a minor intrusion, and it is easy to overlook it, and see all that lies beyond.

One of the first hills in what is often referred to as The Ettrick Horseshoe is the hill with two names. On the early maps it is given as The Pen of Eskdalemuir, whereas the Ordnance Survey has it as Ettrick Pen. This puzzling difference is most likely simply down to the direction from which the respective surveyors approached it. Eskdale claimed it as theirs and then some time later, the people of Ettrick clearly regarded it as *their* Pen. With the remains of an

**Towards Moffat From
Chalk Rig Edge**
Cloud wisps and snow
shaddow draw the eye
down Annan Water from the
heights of Chalk Rigg Edge
towards Moffat.
David Lintern
NT078134

contrast, to the left is the first serious object lesson in glaciation on and around the Watershed. Four great buttresses point boldly towards the long straight and deep valley of the Moffat Water. Between, and on either side of Swatte Fell, Saddle Yoke, Carrifran Gans and White Coomb are deeply and steeply carved valleys. This is surely the place from which to view them – they may look impressive, domineering even, from the road that runs along the valley floor, but their full grandeur can only be fully appreciated from this high vantage point. The full drama is completed with the backdrop to this, Hart Fell, Firthhope Rigg, and Lochcraig Head forming the skyline.

The turning point is reached at Herman Law, where a farewell is bid to the Ettrick Horseshoe, and a steep descent must be taken to Birkhill, at the watershed between Yarrow with St Mary's Loch, and Moffat Water. Charles Lapworth stayed at Birkhill during his fieldwork which led to the discovery and examination of graptolite fossils at nearby Dob's Linn. These discoveries played a major part in helping to unravel the puzzle of the origin and movement of rocks and in the development of the discipline of geology. Birkhill is the only house right on the Reiver March of the Watershed.

Of the thousands of visitors who look up in admiration from the rock below to the Grey Mare's Tail, a number then venture up to Loch Skeen to appreciate this picturesque high level body of water. The Watershed sweeps round the boundary of this National Trust for Scotland property, by Watch Knowe, above the loch, to Lochcraig Head. By-passing White Coomb, the highest hill in the area, it then skirts the upper reaches of the Borders Forest Trust's (BFT) inspirational project area, the Carrifran Wildwood. A good view of this is had from up here at Rotten Bottom – an area of serious peat hag. This great project, aims to re-create a wild wood as it would have been some 6,000 years ago. The ever popular Hart Fell is now firmly in sight.

The Devil's Beef Tub comes into view at the western end of a line of hills marking the very headwaters of the River Tweed to the right, and dropping steeply by some 500m to the left at the start of the Annan Water. Here at Corehead, the BFT is pursuing its

Talla Nick to Loch Skeen

From a drift and a dyke at
Talla Nick, Loch Skeen holds
a cold high crag-girt vigil in the
hills, on this occasion.

David Lintern

NT158169

ancient cairn on its summit, it must have had some significance to
our distant ancestors.

The route swings round clockwise, above the headwaters
by Ettrick Head, where the Southern Upland Way crosses,
Portpatrick some distance to the left, and Cockburnspath a
slightly shorter walk to the right. Either of the hills at this
extremity of the valley will repay many times over the time given
to stopping to admire the view in a wide arc from east to west,
by way of south. The Lakeland Fells are becoming less distinct,
but the Solway and Galloway coast mark a clear line between sea
and land. If conditions are clear, the Isle of Man may even put in
a vague appearance. A steeply eroded valley around Croft Head is
fine indeed, and the Great Wall of Ettrick emerges shortly after
Capel Fell.

Bodesbeck Law marks the start of a very fine ridge, running
along the crest of the valley of Moffat Water, with six named tops
on it. To the right, a series of short spurs leading off down into
Ettrick like a succession of rounded waves, and with views back
across to Ettrick Pen and her neighbours to be enjoyed. In marked

second great ancient forest regeneration project. Crossing by the
A701 just beyond Flecket Hill, a brief forest section then brings
the route to Clyde Law, where a wind farm reminds us of this form
of intrusion, the unwelcome industrial exploitation of wilder
countryside.

Tweedsmuir Hills

A short final section of the Reiver March turns sharply north at
Clyde Law along the Tweedsmuir Hills and thus provides a sense
of the real purpose and direction of the Watershed, a northwards
journey. The litany of 16 named tops carries the route to Culter
Fell. From there, the end of this March is almost in sight, at
Gawky Hill on the lip of the Southern Uplands Fault line.

As a first foray onto the Watershed of Scotland, the Reiver
March will have provided a fine mix of diversity, challenge and
delight. It has however been a relatively gentle introduction. It will
hopefully have stimulated a growing enjoyment of this immense
geographic feature, and the engagement with Nature which can
grow from this.

Peter Wright

Black Law From The Bell

Late afternoon winter sky over
the south Pentlands gives this
vista from The Bell to Black
Law a dramtic effect.
David Lintern
NT111502

Chapter Three	The Laich March – *Linking Wildness with Wildness*

Nature is always lovely, invincible, glad,
whatever is done and suffered by her creatures.
All scars she heals, whether in rocks or water
or sky or hearts. JOHN MUIR

The concept of viewing and experiencing a part of the Scottish landscape, which is casually crossed and recrossed by thousands of people by road and rail every day, from an entirely new perspective is radical. The central belt, the waistline of Scotland, is seen by most as that industrial swathe stretching between the Glasgow and Edinburgh areas on a simple west – east orientation. Much of the population of Scotland lives within this strip of the country, which is around 80 miles long and 30 miles wide. Generally lower lying, its geology provided the rich resources of coal, shale and iron, needed to generate and sustain a range of industries. Indeed, the industrial revolution took a powerful hold in this area. Although the heavy industries have all but vanished, other services have replaced them, and the area still includes much of the most populated and economically active in the country.

The geology of Scotland appears to put a particular perspective on this area, and its hinterland. Scotland is the sum of its parts. Two major fault lines cut a duo of clear and straight lines on a south-west to north-east orientation, and mark the boundaries of the *geological central belt*. The more southerly of these is the Southern Upland Fault, already referred to as the terminus of the Reiver March on Gawky Hill. This runs from Ballantrae in the south-west to Dunbar in the east. The ground elevation to the north of this fault line, on the Watershed, is almost 300m lower than that to the south. Some 90km as the crow flies to the north of this, is the Highland Boundary Fault line, which runs definitively from Bute to Stonehaven, in exactly the same south-west to north-east orientation, and parallel to its' southerly counterpart.

Tarbrax Panorama
Distant industrial use of the landscape both past and present, is out-done by closer wildness at Crosswoodhill.
Keith Brame
NT034561

In Carron Valley
The margins of the Carron Valley Resevoir in the Campsie Fells exude the abundance and appeal of Nature.

Mary Bates,
Balfron Heritage Trust
NS681855

Fannyside Loch

Close to Cumbernauld, Fannyside Loch is almost surrounded by valuable and protected ornithological habitiats.

Peter Wright
NT798737

Tinto Framed by Biggar Common Beech Trees

Familiar landmarks like Tinto take on a new delight when framed by this Biggar Common woodland.

Peter Woolverton
NT021379

Below

Craigengar from Little King Seat

Rough grazing, open moor and woodland mingle under an appealing sky, from Little King Seat to Craigengar.

David Lintern
NT129523

The transition from Reiver to Laich as you cross the Southern Upland Fault to Coulter just south of Biggar, and the notable reduction in elevation which this brings, gives a hint at the significance of the word *laich*, which simply means *low* in the Scots vernacular. Although the geological Fault lines are only 90km apart, the March takes a much less direct 190km to make this journey. Emptiness is almost the norm, with a mere handful of houses, and only one settlement directly on the route. Four churches and mosque are adjacent, and a Roman Altar Stone is the precursor to the crossing by the Antonine Wall. It is criss-crossed by road, rail and canal, and the end of the Cumbernauld Airport runway just touches upon it. Fourteen designated sites are to be found on and about the line, and a number of key environmental organisations play an active part in this, and other habitat conservation. Although the Laich March may lack the dramatic landscape features and the habitats found on much of the rest

Forth and Clyde Canal
Forth and Clyde Canal provides
scope for varied recreation,
and with protected marshlands
beyond the far shore.
Peter Wright
NS758782

of the Watershed, it is nonetheless a green, if work-worn link
between Reiver and Heartland. It contains much that enriches the
lives of people living locally; and, as will be seen, has tantalising
potential for good.

Biggar Common

The first 25km of this March, running from the summit of Gawky
Hill to the summit of Black Mount, is very varied in character
and terrain. Hill, moor, rough grazing, field and forest are all
represented here. Although there are areas of field, the margins of
this cultivation are marked by hedgerow and woodland, providing
a mixed habitat, rich in wildlife. Biggar Common gives fine views
over the surrounding countryside – south to the hills around
Culter Fell, south-west to the ever popular Tinto, west across the
Clyde Valley, north into the Pentland Hills, and east across the
Tweed Valley to Broughton Heights, so beloved of the author John
Buchan. Biggar herself nestles below, with spire, and a random

Kippen Muir

Stronend in the north western corner of the Fintry Hills watches benignly over Kippen Muir.
Peter Wright
NS613921

jumble of roofs and chimneys, so evocative of an old and homely community.

The route then wends its way to the ancient cairn and embankments of Hyndshawland, which is surrounded by a Christmas tree farm. Black Mount, a long whaleback of a hill follows, across heather moor, which in season is a blaze of purple. From this vantage point, the next target can be seen, across the wooded Garvald, to the southern end of the Pentland Hills.

South Pentland

The Pentland Hills, which Stevenson fondly called 'The Hills of Home', have been immensely popular for generations of Edinburgh residents. But they tend to confine their walks to the higher, more distinctive northern end of this small range, leaving the gentler southern part to only the more adventurous. The Watershed here crosses from The Bell on Mendick Hill, to Henshaw Hill above Bawdy Moss, by way of Craigengar. This

Coulter Kirk
The interesting shape of Coulter Kirk sits upon the Watershed amid ancient graveyard and woodland setting.
Ruth Longmuir, Borders Exploration.
NT027342

modest hill with its twin cairns and inscribed boulder is however no ordinary hill, for it marks a number of things. It is the end of the Tweed catchment as far as the Watershed of Scotland is concerned, at least. It marks the start of the huge area in the central belt which is the province of the Central Scotland Forest Trust (CSFT), and has both SSSI and SAC status. A pause to take in the view will easily justify the delay in the journey, for the business of trying to identify many familiar everyday landmarks from this vantage, is intriguing.

Descending to Bawdy Moss (another SSSI), the Laich March does indeed appear to be *low* as it crosses moor and rough grazing just above Tarbrax, Cobbinshaw Reservoir and Woolfords. A wind-farm now dominates the scene ahead, before Hendry's Corse, and then the route re-enters the commercial forest. This whole section of the Watershed is probably amongst the most troubled, and environmentally oppressed. Scrappy forest, land-fill site and the prospect of a waste incinerator close-by, another very large wind farm around Black Law, semi-reinstated opencast extraction, unsightly fly tipping, and the remnants of coal mining, all combine to make the green thread all but invisible. Amongst all

Towards Biggar Common from Shaw Hill

Biggar Common from Shaw Hill, with the town sitting comfortably in a wooded landscape.

Peter Woolverton
NT043345

this however, habitat regeneration and management, two sssi's of active bog, planting of native species woodland, and even areas of gentle neglect – paradoxically bringing a positive habitat recovery, all combining to produce a sense of optimism.

Black Law and Cant Hills

This very mixed picture continues across to Fannyside Loch on the edge of Palacerigg Country Park. For every negative, there is a positive, and it would seem that the latter is winning through – just. It is to be hoped that the new attention which is slowly being focussed upon the Watershed, and its immense potential for people's health and wellbeing as well as the wildlife enhancement, will all add to a turning of the environmental tide in the central belt. No other continuous geographic and landscape feature that is in turn visibly connected to such a large part of the wider Scottish landform carries such current and potential positive bearing.

Two railways now cross the route in this stretch near Tarbothie Farm and Forrestfield, and traffic on the m8 Motorway plies its way across near Kirk of Shotts. The transmitter mast of the same name soars skyward, and her two neighbours at Blackhill on the north side of the Motorway combine to provide huge visual markers, both day and night. An assortment of quarries,

both active and redundant, and a prominent hilltop water works all contribute to the rather industrial look of parts of this area. Amongst it all however, patches of native woodland planting, natural regeneration and protected active bog, all serve to redress the picture – for wildlife, and our enjoyment of it.

Cumbernauld

Palacerigg Country Park is a popular destination for people living in the Cumbernauld area; it is a haven for wildlife. From Fannyside Loch with all of the designations it carries, for water fowl in particular, through the mature woodlands of the Park, and the more open clearings, blossoms abound and birdsong is fulsome.

There are those who scoff at Cumbernauld as a New Town and urban development, but the Watershed's eye view of the town is nonetheless very green. As the line of the Watershed weaves round and about the flats, warehouses, churches, schools and all that makes up the built fabric of the place, it quite magically links so many areas of woodland – old and more recent, hedgerow, and other evidence of greenery.

Kilsyth and Fintry Hills

The ascent to Tomtain in the Kilsyth Hills heralds a 41km stretch of hill and moor, with a few areas of forest, and one wind farm. The most powerful pleasures in this are the views and the vivid sense of place, which these generate. Almost the entire central belt is laid-out beyond the base of these hills, and much time can be most enjoyably dallied away, picking out features which somehow shrink into the wider landscape from this perspective.

The first part of this section is the sweep round the headwaters

On Biggar Common
Sheep and young lambs dot the fields bounded by mature beech trees on Biggar Common.
Peter Woolverton
NT019382

Below
Biggar Rooftops from Biggar Common
Jumbeld roofscapes of the ancient burgh of Biggar are glimpsed through the trees of The Knock on Biggar Common.
Peter Woolverton
NT032378

of the River Carron, with its reservoir filling the valley bottom below. This takes the route west into the very heart of the Campsie Fells at Holehead, followed by a sweep east past the end of the Reservoir, the scant remains of Sir Roger de Graham's castle, and onto Cairnoch Hill. This last may involve a bit of a battle with the trees. The wind farm on Hart Hill is an uncompromising intrusion onto the Watershed. Thankfully however, once that is behind, the promise of the stunning views from Carleatheran, become the widening focus of attention. Take time here to pause and ponder, and to try to identify some of the jagged peaks on the skyline of The Trossachs across the headwaters of the Forth. An easy descent to the vicinity of the Spout of Ballochleam is followed by a steady climb to Stronend, or *the end of the nose.*

Balgair Muir and Bat a Charchel

Getting safely down from the heights of Stronend in the north western corner of the Fintry Hills, should be delayed briefly at least, in order, once again, to take in the scenic splendour. Ben Lomond, upper Forth Valley, and a large number of the

hills around Ben Vorlich mark out some of the best in the Loch Lomond and Trossachs National Park – but with the exception of the big Loch herself, for that will come slightly later in this saga.

Care is needed in this descent, for in places, the ground is both steep and loose, so the advice is to focus on the task at foot, and not the view.

The next 21km is, like the start of this March, across very varied terrain – in that familiar litany of bog, moor, forest and field. Guilann, on the Highland Boundary Fault, north-east of Balmaha on Loch Lomond, is the goal. The route will touch upon Kippen Muir, Ballindalloch Muir, skirt close to Balfron, and following Camoquhill, which means *top of the hill*, be crossed by what is left of the Bog of Ballat. A gentle climb across rough fields, past areas of mature woodland interspersed with hedgerow and course-grazing, brings the route to Bat a Charchel, with its dominant communication mast. Leaving that behind, and passing Muir Park Reservoir, the route leads onto the heather clad and flowing lines of Moor Park and Tom nam Broc, the *little hill of the badger*. A short steep ascent then brings the fulfilling rewards of the summit of Guilann.

Canada Geese on Black Loch

These canada geese have taken up residence here on Black Loch, close to Limerigg.

Peter Wright

NS856699

The Laich March has magically carried this resilient green thread through some of the most unlikely of locations: places where it does take a positive environmental attunement to appreciate that it is there, and that it is real. It has also linked a significant number of important designated and protected sites, and has provided a genuine ribbon that binds the areas of open moor and hill, the bog and the native woodland together. It has demonstrated, the immense value of the work of the Central Scotland Forest Trust, and others in the greening of the central belt, with the Laich March, more by chance than design, at the heart of it.

There is much to be done however to drive this forward, and realise the aspirations of a small but growing number of people – both local, and from further of the area. There is much that can be done to exploit the potential which this undoubtedly has in strengthening this Scotland-long ribbon of wildness, not least where it spans that most populated part of the country. Some form of designation and protection would help. That indeed, should

Natural Regeneration on Longriggend Moor

Early in last century this area near Longriggend was torn apart by mining activity, today it is within Nature's dominion.

Peter Wright
NS815696

be the objective, but may yet be some way off. There is much that could be done to make the local authorities in the area more aware of it, and begin to bring it more coherently into their respective Biodiversity Action Plans. There are also a number of other organisations, both national and local that can build upon the part that they already play, in one way or another.

Recent developments in the educational world, with the growing implementation of Curriculum for Excellence, affecting all school sectors, provides a golden opportunity to utilise the Watershed, and the Laich March part of it in particular, for educational purposes. The potential impact of children and young people on *their* environment and landscape is almost limitless. There are plenty of good examples within the environmental and educational fields, both statutory and voluntary, to demonstrate the *how* and the *why*, *and* to show that it can work, and work well – both for the young people and the projects that they may engage in. There are also the means to give this activity structure and purpose in the form of recognition, through the John Muir

Palacerigg Country Park

The people of Cumbernauld are proud of their own Palacerigg Country Park, where wildlife abounds.

David MacFarlane, Palacerigg Country Park

NS787732

Below

Across Upper Forth Valley From Carleatheran

Upper Forth Valley and The Trossachs stretch enticingly in mellow mood beyond Carleatheran in the Gargunnock Hills.

Peter Wright

NS687918

Award and other such programmes. Partnership is powerful. Organisations working together can achieve much more than plodding on in isolation. Some, at least, of the necessary adult training to facilitate this is in place, and every organisation which might conceivably be involved, will already have all of the necessary Health and Safety procedures.

This optimism is underpinned by the author's own experience over many years, of quite simply making these kind of things happen elsewhere in Scotland. How then can this educational potential in the Watershed locally be carried forward, and turned into an active, creative reality?

Jim Shedden

Jim Shedden

Ben Alder

No better vantage for the
mass of Ben Alder, than across
Bealach Beithe from the
northern end of Beinn
Bheoil ridge.
Nick Bramhall
NN469718

Chapter Four

The Heartland March – *Cresting the Mountains Beyond the Highland Line*

The mountains are fountains of men as well as of rivers, of glaciers, of fertile soil. The great poets, philosophers, prophets, able men whose thoughts and deeds have moved the world have come down from the mountains – mountain dwellers who have grown strong there with the forest trees in Nature's workshops. JOHN MUIR

Our epic trail now crests the tops and high bealachs along the skyline of some of the most familiar and loved landscapes in the country. This is the Scotland celebrated in song and verse, and on the itinerary of so many tours and journeys. It epitomises all that is best in selling Scotland, stirring the emotions and creating a profound nostalgia for the entire body of Scotland's long diaspora. Great lochs and mountains, valleys and forests, legend and awakening of the imagination, all combine to provide images of landscape which exude the romantic spirit.

Scott and Stevenson, those giants of Scottish literature, wove this scenery into their works, and used it to good effect to add drama and atmosphere to their stories. The nostalgic chorus at least, of that famous refrain about the *Bonnie Banks*, is known and sung the world over, and regarded by many as something that is firmly rooted in the place that it brings so strongly to life. Over 30,000 people a year are drawn to climb Ben Lomond, making it one of the most popular of our higher mountains. The numbers and diversity of people that visit the area generates such pressure on the very sites they have come to admire, that visitor management and specific by-laws, have now been enacted.

The word 'romantic' has a fitting resonance for the location, its place in literature and its association with some of the great historical characters who came from or roamed these hills. Visitors can walk in the footsteps

Black Mount from Loch Ba

Ever a photographers' favourite, the arc of mountains of the Black Mount reflected in the waters of Loch Ba.

Keith Brame
NN323500

In Cashel Forest
The emerging Cashel Forest is the Royal Scottish Forestry Society's millenium project, rising from lochside to hilltop.
Mary Bates,
Balfron Heritage Trust
NS409953

Below
Cruach Ardrain
A bold pace and snow-tracks mark the pace towards the ragged summits of Cruach Ardrain and her neighbours.
Keith Brame
NN409212

of the outlaw Rob Roy MacGregor for he now has a trail named after him, to facilitate such a following. Although Rannoch Moor is now skirted in part by a busy main road, it still evokes a true sense of wildness and on a murky day, even the kind of terror that the Romantic Movement so avidly sought. Neighbouring Glen Coe fires the imagination, with the tradition of massacre and betrayal, and with spectacular precipice and ridge which set the heart racing, even when viewed from the safety of the roadside. In a bold attempt to subdue the natives following '45, Wade and

Caulfield were commissioned to construct a great network of military roads and bridges throughout much of the Highlands. There is still evidence of this engineering to be found in many of the glens hereabouts.

One of the greats of Celtic legend, Ossian has a loch named after him here, and its setting can

only be described as stunning. The remotest railway station in the country is located in the middle of a moor which overlooks Loch Ossian, with no public road access, and no settlement, the train simply sets the traveller down *in the middle of nowhere*. But that very *nowhere* has a breath-taking wild beauty and splendour.

Loch Ericht and Beyond from Ben Alder

The south end of Loch Ericht from Ben Alder, is but the precursor to a long bold southerly skyline of fine mountains.

Fraser McAlistair
NN496718

Scotland currently has just two National Parks, in the forms of The Trossachs and Loch Lomond, and The Cairngorm. Both cover areas of the country which are hugely popular among our own population and foreign visitors alike. Their landscapes are iconic, by any standards. As National Parks and their respective Authorities, both are relatively young, and in some senses still establishing their respective roles, and the functions they serve for landscape, people and economic activity. But what links and connects them physically, is quite literally, as old as the hills; it is Nature's own 'ribbon of wildness' no less. Our trail goes right through the middle of the former of these designated areas, and touches gently on the western fringes of the latter.

The places in which road, rail and way-marked walking routes cross and re-cross the Watershed may be familiar for very large numbers of travellers, but stray just a short distance from these crossings, and it is peace that prevails. Venture just a little further again, and it is remoteness with all the solitude that this can bring, which is assured for the lover of wild places. Wildness is the anchor that transcends all of these manufactured ways.

Loch Lomond Islands

The young trees on the slopes of Cashel provide a fine setting from which to survey the Loch Lomond islands.

Mary Bates,
Balfron Heritage Trust
NS432926

Our high-level trail encompasses a list of significant sites and associations, including two National Nature Reserves, the active work of big National and voluntary environmental organisations, and the creative partnerships which they have forged by working together. As the people of Glasgow and much of the urban West of Scotland turn on their taps, the water that pours out will have been collected first in Loch Katrine and her neighbouring reservoirs. This entire water catchment area is managed in order to ensure a high-quality supply can be provided. What is good for the water supply will almost certainly be excellent for wildlife too. One of the big estates has radically altered its ways of working, and with the active support of the John Muir Trust, it has put biodiversity to the fore, and commercial deer stalking has been demoted. Significant managed reduction in deer numbers on Corrour Estate is beginning to make way for natural regeneration of many native species.

The Heartland March can therefore be shown to carry the Watershed through some of Scotland's finest and most widely appreciated landscapes, with a rich mix of the dramatic, the

remote, the familiar and the popular mountain areas. What the Laich March may have lacked in rugged splendour, is more than compensated for hereabouts.

The average elevation of this March at some 610m above sea level is a good 330m (over 1,000 feet) higher than Laich. With a length of just over 250km, it carries the Watershed from within 30 km from the centre of Glasgow, to the centre of the Great Glen; worlds apart.

Trossachs

Standing on the summit of Guilann just to the East of Balmaha, and near the bottom right-hand corner of Loch Lomond, the familiar and entirely appealing theme of a sense of place is strong. The vista to the west is dominated by Loch Lomond, the largest sheet of fresh water in Scotland. Conic Hill to the south-west points the eye to a string of four islands in the Loch, which clearly illustrate the line of the Highland Boundary Fault, with Ben Bowie as its marker on the western shore. Turning the other way, the line is harder to pick out of the dark green spread of Loch Ard Forest, but beyond Aberfoyle it becomes much clearer in the form of the Menteith Hills. This division of the Watershed into five Marches on the Scottish Mainland, by using these geological fault lines as the points of transition from one to the other makes perfect sense, in terms of both the country's physical structure, and its habitat characteristics.

Ben Lomond is the dominant feature to the north-west, and before it a succession of hills neatly marks the boundary between a forest landscape to the right, and one that is loch-bound on the left. It is surprising to find that this string of hills before Ben Lomond is evidently not walked more often. The absence

Loch Laggan from Above Coire Ardair
In a turmoil of cloud and sunlight Loch Laggan gives some back in this eye-catching vista from high on Coire Ardair.
Keith Brame
NN437892

Below
Pol-gormack Hill
The going is slow and difficult across the peat-hags which dominate the terrain to the west of Pol-gormack Hill.
Richard Webb,
Geograph protocol
NN390979

Loch Lochy from Creag an Gobhar

Creag nan Gobhar provides a splendid vantage point for Loch Lochy, and the snow capped peaks to the north.

Kirsty Bloom,
Great Glen Hostel
NN315984

Beinn Dubhchraig and Loch Lomond
Watershed-runner Colin Meek, on Beinn Dubhchraig, with Glen Falloch and Loch Lomond as backdrop.
Chris Dyer
NN308253

Below
From Beinn Bheag to The Auch Loop
Mountains around Auch loop include Beinn Dorain and Beinn a Chaisteal, form a fine group viewed from Bein Bheag.
Peter Wright
NN315325

of any clear path along much of the ridge, suggests that these are overlooked by most walkers, in favour of the much larger neighbour. If increasing numbers of people were to venture to walk these parts of the Watershed though, it would open up the delights of the evolving panorama across the Loch, and over the upper headwaters of the Forth. It would also give that great experience of a sense of anticipation prior to the ascent of the Ben.

Beinn a Chreachain Towards Beinn Achaladair

The swing east gives a fine perspective on Beinn Achaladair from its near neighbour Beinn a Chreachain.

James Wright
NN372441

Most people who do climb Ben Lomond do so from Rowardennan by the well-constructed and maintained path which ensures that all this foot traffic doesn't destroy the mountain. A few do however climb up from the Loch Ard side by way of the Gleann Dubh. Both routes merge on the Watershed at Moin Each, which then follows close to the path to the summit.

The descent is to the more rugged north-west, to Cruachan on the south side of Loch Arklet. Beinn a Choin can be seen directly to the north beyond the far side of Glen Arklet, but the journey there, involves a 5km sweep to the east before dropping down to the narrow strip of land between Lochs Arklet and Katrine. A steep crag and scrub-girt ascent follows, giving perhaps the first real such experience on the entire Watershed, and helping to establish the character of the Heartland March. Seven marked tops carry the trail north-west, before a descent to the very head of Glen Gyle, with its unflattering line of electricity pylons which carry the power from distant Cruachan on Loch Awe. This same rugged terrain continues across by Parlan Hill to Sron Garbh, where an entirely new vista has opened up, with Crianlarich to the north, and some 550m below. From here, the Heartland March however misses the village by about a kilometre, and swings sharply to the west to take in an exceptionally fine clutch of mountains in which Ben Lui is chief.

Lui and Grampian

These mountains are all highly popular and well-climbed in all seasons, with Crianlarich at the hub of several potentially good days out. Those ahead and on the Watershed offer an exceptional

if demanding day, which has the advantage of public transport at both ends to make it all the more practical. The surrounding landscapes are special, with one of the National Nature Reserves just below to the right. Each of the mountains and tops has its own special character, whether deeply cut by glacial scouring, long shoulders of ascent, or ragged steep descents which need care and courage. It is not surprising that the image of this jagged skyline, when captured from some other vantage is instantly recognisable, for those who have ventured to experience all that these peaks have to offer. Mining for gold and other precious metals will resume beneath these hills in the near future, and while this may appear to be an inappropriate development in such a fine scenic area, the conditions being imposed are rigorous.

A succession of railways, 'A' roads and the West Highland Way (WHW) crossings bring the route briefly into the province of busier travel. This is followed by a relentless 600m ascent onto Beinn Odhar and then a series of rounded grassy tops running north, close to the western end of Loch Lyon, and onto Beinn Achaladair. A long sweep east is bold and clear above the deep valley of Tulla Water to the left, and Loch Lyon closely hugging the hills to the right. The terrain for some of this stretch is craggier, with one, sharply ice-scooped, corrie lochan several hundred metres below to the left. On Creag Mhor the expanse of Rannoch Moor spreads out in all its watery wonder to the north, a feature which will dominate for well over the next 60km. With a final flourish in this swing eastwards the trail to distant Meall Buidhe is reached, followed by an acute angled turn north to the head of Rannoch Forest where another railway crossing appears.

Ben Alder
The ice-sculpted form of Ben
Alder catches a little morning
sunlight in this appealing view
from around Culra.
Fraser McAlistair
NN469718

Round Rannoch

The clockwise circumnavigation
of Rannoch Moor starts on Meall
a Ghortain – the Heartland March
takes some 55km to accomplish
the rim of this vast moor, which
is as much open water as firm
terrain. The final departure from this is a mere 12km to the north,
close to the snow shed beyond Rannoch Station on the west
Highland Line. This is however a spectacular demonstration of
the hand of Nature, for She, and She alone formed the line of the
Watershed, and in a grand gesture determined where the higher
ground on the rim should be. During the last Ice Age, a dome of
ice almost two kilometres in thickness spread across this area and
from this a number of glaciers radiated outwards. These in turn
scoured, gouged and sculpted the landform we see today. When
the ice finally retreated, the entire land surface rose significantly,
as if in a sigh of relief perhaps, at the removal of such a heavy
burden.

The Rannoch Rim starts with some innocuous hills and moor
running along the north side of Tulla, but the craggy descent
from Glas Bheinn to the A82 heralds much sterner stuff. The
Black Mount loosely defines the area around the head of the River
Ba, which is in turn at the western extremity of the longest river
in Scotland, the Tay. Salt water at the head of Loch Etive is but
11km west of Stob Ghabhar – here, the Watershed almost has a
toe on the Atlantic side. This tight collection of mountain terrain
is rough, challengingly steep in parts, and streaked with scree in
others. An easier descent to the next WHW and A82 re-crossings,
gives time to ponder the route across a tricky and featureless part
of the Moor, to Black Corries Lodge. Getting this right is essential,
for to miss the one narrow *bridge* of firm, flat but dry moor, would
court the need for a long and frustrating detour, or indulging in
the bog-hopping reel.

Black Corries Lodge is a mere 200m from the Watershed, and
is only the second such structure on the entire Heartland March.

A track runs invitingly up to the north-east, but our trail carries on north onto a shoulder of Meall nan Ruadhag before swinging due east onto and along A Chruach. The retreating ice left a scatter of boulders on this ridge, and now they sit, casually abandoned among the heather. The descent to the north-east is by way of the Glac Dhubh, and yet another railway crossing just north of the snow shed. With another area of very flat and watery terrain to be crossed, Sron a Leachd Chaorainn is the clear goal, at the start of a memorable ridge running north, and culminating in Carn Dearg.

Corrour and Alder

Ascending the ridge leading up to Carn Dearg develops a very fine sense of anticipation, and the views are well worthy of a tea break. To the south, the vista extends back across Rannoch Moor to Beinn Achaladair, and the entire ridge on the north side of Loch Lyon. Turning clockwise, the dramatic skyline is formed with the Black Mount and Buachaille Etive Mor, and merging into the ragged profile of the back, or north side, of Aonach Eagach above Glen Coe. The surface of the Blackwater Reservoir catches the afternoon light as it snakes its way westwards to fade into the haze. The immense mountain mass that includes Ben Nevis brings the panorama round, with peak superimposed on peak – the nearer the clearer, while the more distant ones fade into infinity. Some smaller rounded hills around Beinn na Lap offer contrast and variety, so the final parts of the ridge fully occupies, for a while, at least the mind and attention.

At the huge, well-built cairn on the summit of Carn Dearg, another pause is called for, because Loch Ossian has now come into view several hundred meters below. Somewhere amongst the few pine trees at the far end lies the Youth Hostel and the track snakes its way across the moor from there to the white dot that is Corrour Station. Whether Ossian ever made it to these parts is lost in the mists, but the wonder of the place is captivating nonetheless. A succession of tops then leads on to the Bealach Cumhann, and a relentless ascent to the great plateau of the summit of Ben Alder.

There is something remarkable about Ben Alder. Remote, it most certainly is, for it takes a bit of effort to get to it from any

Ben Lomond

Ever popular and iconic
Ben Lomond lies at the very
heart of the surrounding
National Park.
NTS photo library
NS350990

Meall Buidhe to Beinn Achaladair

The snow-clad northern face of Meall Buidhe provides a bold spectacle overlooking Tulla Water.

Andy Hunter, Geograph protocol NN352439

direction. It stands out amongst all of its neighbours, and offers views that are truly majestic. Almost ringed with formidable crags, the routes both up and down need to be chosen with care. Viewed from any perspective, it is a massive mountain. The highly distinctive form of Schiehallion can just be recognised to the south, Dalwhinnie and the traffic on the A9 can be picked out beyond the end of Loch Ericht, and all around are mountain groups, some familiar, some less so, with the light on random lochs to break up the prevailing solid vistas. Descending slowly towards Beinn Bheoil, you become aware of its very rough whaleback form, which both contrasts with the flat surface of Loch Ericht, and yet somehow matches its long narrow shape.

Whether Culra Bothy is the planned shelter for the night or not, it is nonetheless, close to this the Heartland March – albeit on the wrong side of the Allt a Chaoil-reidhe, which empties just three kilometres downstream into Loch Pattack. The Watershed here is marked by two very gently rounded areas of (wet) moorland, the second of which, Meall Beag, is followed by a track crossing and a gap in, a strip of commercial forest, leading onto the start of The Fara ridge of hills, but the trail quickly swings north to Beinn Eilde.

Laggan

From this modest top, a new vista is revealed. To the north, the
Monadhliaths roll into the distance, while the village of Laggan
nestles in the Spey Valley in the foreground. Now this marks a
major milestone on the trail, for the Spey drains northwards,
and empties into the Moray Firth. Loch Laggan can be seen to
the north-west, with the immense bulk of Creag Meagaidh as
backdrop. Although it is not quite on the trail, the Dark Gully is
worth a slight detour, and then the forest beckons – fine mature
pine with few low branches to obstruct the way, and grass
underfoot. Another detour is called for shortly, as a fast-flowing
concrete-lined water channel, to capture the waters of the Mashie
and empty them into the Pattack at Feagour, runs right across the
way. Laggan Forest Trust is doing much to maximise the benefit
the forest can bring to the local community. This initiative was the
brainchild of a local resident who was concerned that large areas
of Forestry Commission estate seemed to bring no jobs or benefit
whatever to the local community. So, he resolved to do something
practical about it, and formed the Trust. The Forest was duly
purchased and is now generating significant local activity.

Creag Ruadh must be climbed through forest and by crag – it does look strangely daunting from level of the A86 crossing, but as is so often the case, the prospect looks much worse than the reality. The trig point at 622 gives the direction for rounding the head of Loch a Lairige on the western side of the hill. Traversing the upper limits of the very short Glen Shirra, and a heart-racing ascent to Meall Ghoirleig, is followed by a rapid 'S' in the trail along the Cairngorm National Park boundary, onto A Bhuidheanach and to the summit of Carn Liath. Here, the view backs east along the stony crest of the mountain draws the eye into the Southern Cairngorms. This is amazingly only about the half-way mark on the mainland, of this epic journey, a long way, it would seem, from Peel Fell on the Border, an equally long way, as yet, to the Duncansby Head in the far north-east – and yet further to achieve that coveted view of Muckle Flugga. But make time here to savour the views, enjoy the panoramas, and take in the place in a wider landscape.

Spey Roy

To the south-east the famous Coire Ardair provides a perfect foreground for Creag Meagaidh. Our route will however narrowly miss that great mountain and turn north on the lower top of Stob

Loch Spey With Carn Liath
Bold crags on and around Carn Liath give the backdrop to the more modest scale of Loch Spey, source of a fine river.
John Ferguson, Geograph protocol NN421943

Poite Coire Ardair, lower than Creag Meagaidh by a mere two metres. This turning is but two kilometres from Loch Roy, at the very head of the River Roy, which flows into the Glen of the same name, with its intriguing formations of the Parallel Roads. The descent northwards continues by Meall Ptarmigan and Sron Nead, with an exhilarating clamber down to another bog. Here the route is marked by a fence, or the remains of one, as it appears to be slowly sinking into the damp vegetation and whatever lies beneath the surface. Just before the Coll on the ancient path between the upper Spey Valley on the right, and the upper reaches of Glen Roy on the left, is Loch Spey – just one kilometre from that sinking fence. This unassuming little body of water, no bigger than a lochan, is the genesis of one of the finest rivers in the country. Such is the power of the Spey when in flood further downstream, that its exit into the Moray Firth at Spey Bay has defied all attempts to tame it. As each Winter it brings down a hefty cargo of pebbles and rock, it unpredictably alters its exit to the Firth by several metres. Out of small lochans, great rivers grow.

Beyond the path crossing at the Coll, a succession of modest enough hills take the Heartland March on a sweep or two to Pollgormack Hill, and on the way, within shouting distance of the Corrieyairack Pass, and General Wade's most ambitious military road, crossing the hills at 780m. Although it is now thankfully restricted to travel on foot only, it remains a formidable piece of engineering well over 200 years after its construction. The infamous Beauly to Denny power line 'upgrade' passes this way too, and it will surely go down as one of the great environmental mistakes. Future generations will wonder what possessed this one to do what it has done. The John Muir Trust and others fought a noble fight to prevent this, and their well-argued case for wiser alternatives will not be forgotten.

From Pol-gormack Hill the Watershed then turns sharply to the west, and starts its 50km trek to Sgurr na Ciche in the Rough Bounds.

Pol-gormack Hill

A bog, however, provides the opening shot in this huge gesture – another bog in which the scant remains of a fence are being swallowed up. Firmer and steeper ground then prevails in the climb onto yet another Carn Dearg (there are three in this area alone). The magnitude of the Great Glen here becomes fully evident, now a vast 'V' shaped trench some 600m in depth, and around 5km in width rim to rim. To get right down into it at the correct location is a significant challenge, for it will inevitably involve another assault by pine needles. Even to get to Creag nan Gobhar involves either ploughing through the first forest on the way, or a short boggy detour. The target is a point on the towpath of the Caledonian Canal just to the north-east of the point where the Allt an Lagain empties into the canal. Each traveller will most surely work out their own way of achieving this, for there is currently no straightforward way that adheres strictly to the route. Trees, hundreds of them, obstruct the way. The homely and welcome prospect however of a night or two in the Great Glen Hostel will more than compensate.

This Heartland March has been an astonishing journey along the skyline of some of the finest and most loved mountain areas in the country. It has provided a unique opportunity to experience it

Loch Lochy
This parade of mountains rise steep and clear from Loch Lochy with the appeal of sunlight, snow and shaddow.
Kirsty Bloom,
Great Glen Hostel
NN318964

in a new way, and to admire otherwise very familiar sights from a novel perspective. All of the superlatives have been fully justified.

Translating the names of just some of the higher tops gives an intriguing and often vivid insight to how our ancestors viewed their higher ground. It was not without meaning then, and if we take the time to discover and ponder, that significance remains for us now, in the early 21st century. So we have climbed *beacon mountain, mountain of the antler or hawk, the castle, mountain of harm or danger, the high heap or stack of the high part, mountain of the black rock, mountain of the elk or stag, and mountain of the calf.* We continued with *mountain of the soaking field, mountain of the plunderers, peak of the dun corrie, peak of the goats, hill of the roaring, red hill, mountain of the rock or water, mountain of the mouth, grey hill, and peak of the pot of the high corrie.*

This is not an abstract exercise: it offers something very real, tangible and thought-provoking. Heartland embraces a rich cultural and environmental heritage, links both of the National Parks, is touched by a number of popular Long Distance Routes, is traversed by the visionary coast-to-coast corridor of native woodland, and unites a panoply of sites recognised nationally for their quality and value. Heartland has attitude.

The Great Glen Hostel
The setting for The Great Glen Hostel is nothing, if not magestic – and a warm welcome awaits the intrepid traveller.
*Kirsty Bloom,
Great Glen Hostel*
NN295970

Jim Shedden

Jim Shedden

Sgurr a Bhealaich Dhearg
Close to Camban Bothy in the
lee of Ben Attow, the terrain
south to Sgurr a Bhealaich
Dhearg will invigorate.

Richard Kermode,
copyright
NH034145

Chapter Five

The Moine March – *Through the North West*

We are now in the mountains and they are in us,
kindling enthusiasm, making every nerve quiver,
filling every pore and cell in us. JOHN MUIR

Our enjoyment of this journey is greatly enriched by the photographs that a number of very able and generous photographers have kindly provided for *Nature's Peace*. They have created a colourful and often dramatic insight to the ever-unfolding landscapes, and they enable us to imagine ourselves to be out on hill or moor, in a way that words alone cannot begin to achieve. The images in *Nature's Peace* convey both the power and passion of all that the ribbon of wildness can give.

The steady ascent out of the Great Glen past Lochan Diota, which is followed by a hefty 560m ascent onto Ben Tee, is to enter into an altogether new experience. Countless superlatives have already been used to suggest a true flavour of what the Watershed is about, and the special qualities of each of the six very different Marches. Many more will be needed to adequately describe this, the Moine March. At 345km it is the longest, but at an average elevation of 595m, it is not quite the highest. For those who love the mountains of Scotland and the great wild land areas, the Moine March comes with a five-star rating, both in terms of the rugged terrain which it includes and its elevated views into many other iconic areas of the country. To venture onto Moine, is to journey through a continuous swathe of some of the finest terrain in the land. Mention many of these tops and mountain groups to any avid hill or mountain walker, and their eyes will light up.

That these areas should be firmly connected by this major geographic feature adds a new dimension to how they are appreciated. Similarly, that this should all be linked through the

Sgurr nan Ceathreamhnan

Radiating ridges from Sgurr nan Ceathreamhnan invitingly contrast light and shade on steep rough crags.

Stephen Middlemiss, Geograph protocol
NH057227

Coire Glas
To imagine the rugged grandeur of much of Coire Glas being crudely submerged in a reservoir would be anathema.
Kirsty Bloom
NN220947

other Marches, with a single entity running the entire length of the country, is without parallel.

The theme of emptiness prevails here, with not one single house or barn directly on the line – the nearest, and it stands alone in every respect, is a cottage on the A837 east of the Cromalt Hills, some 200m from the Watershed.

One of the big controversies 'which all too often surfaces in heated discussion throughout the north-west' is deer numbers. In the green corner are aligned those who are concerned primarily with the issue of biodiversity, the environmentalists. Whilst in the red corner are arrayed those who are focussed on shooting and the jobs which this sport sustains, the stalker's interests. Although

Sgurr na Ciche
Sgurr nan Coireachan provides
a magnificent vista under an
angry sky to the Garbh Chiochs
and Sgurr na Ciche.
David Lintern
NM902967

debate about this issue is by no means confined to this area, it seems to be most vociferous in the north-west, and many people living locally are enthusiastically allied to one camp or the other.

The name which has been given to this March is drawn from a geological feature which runs prominently from the southern tip of the Island of Skye to the eastern side of Loch Eriboll on the north coast. It dominates the landform along this entire slice of the north-west. This, the *Moine Thrust*, is a gently sloping fault line, in which older rocks have been forced to override much younger ones, creating a layered conundrum. The discovery of the movement of tectonic plates has however demystified this, and provides an explanation.

This process and the evidence of it are best seen at Knockan Crag beside the A835 just south of Elphin. The direct effect of this thrust fault has been that the rocks on the west side of it are entirely different from those on the eastern side.

Having ascended out of the Great Glen, the Watershed then swings directly west for over 40km, and takes it right into an area very aptly called The Rough Bounds. This westward sweep was caused around 400 million years ago, when the whole northern part of what we now call Scotland moved at the Great Glen Fault. The area to the north of this slid in a south-westerly direction, relative to the landmass to the south of the fault line.

A combination of the effects of the two faults has therefore ensured that much of the Watershed in the Moine March is close to the west coast. The Moine Thrust also caused the Scottish landform to tilt, with the west being higher and therefore more rugged than the east, while that slide at the Great Glen, as has been seen, carried it further west. This in turn took it towards the Atlantic seaboard, which is subject to harsh erosion from the prevailing winds and currents from the south-west.

Westward from Tee to Eag

If plans by Scottish and Southern to build the biggest pump
storage hydro electric scheme in the country, in Coire Glas to
the south of Meall a Choire Ghlais, come to pass, it will surely
be one of the greatest contemporary acts of environmental
vandalism imaginable. Lying just south-west of Ben Tee, the *fairy
hill*, this pristine high-level landscape will be destroyed with the
construction of a vast dam, and all of the infrastructure and roads
associated with it. An ever-changing tideline will form along
the shores of the new body of water, and the delicate ecosystem
on scree and steep ground will disappear forever. At the time of
writing, this ill-conceived proposal has been given consent by
Highland Council, as the relevant local authority. It is to be hoped

On South Glen Shiel Ridge
Clean lines of the south face
of South Glen Shiel ridge are
crested with a giant rollercoaster from peak to peak.
Marie Lainton
NG983112

that on account of its scale, it will be called in by the Scottish Government, and come under full scrutiny at a public enquiry. At that point, it will perhaps be seen for what it really is, and roundly rejected.

There is still time, therefore, to climb the perfection of Ben Tee and her neighbours, and to enjoy an unsullied landscape with stunning views and the sense of place, which she so readily affords. The Great Glen and all its grandeur dominates, with Loch Lochy and the mountains around Ben Nevis in one direction, and Lochs Oich and Ness stretching almost endlessly in the other. The vista to the north is over Glen Garry, and to the west along the mountain rollercoaster range which lies ahead, on the next 40km of this great journey. Some of the bealachs to be crossed are deep and steep, and conversely, some of the peaks to be scaled are big and abrupt. It is a section with widely contrasting walking experience, for it even includes an area of Flow, or quaking bog, right on the Watershed, between Sgurr Choinich and Meall Blair. The ever-changing light on those surrounding lochs fully repays the time spent admiring the view, and the sense of increasing ruggedness becomes yet more evident from Sgurr Mhurlagain westwards.

Fraoch Bheinn and Kinbreack Bothy
Kinbreack Bothy in Glen Kingie is dwarfed by neighbouring Watershed hills of Sgurr Mhurlagain and Fraoch Bheinn.
Richard King
NN001916

Rough Bounds

In *Ribbon of Wildness*, I referred to them as '*rocky doodles*' – a fairly graphic description of those places on the map, where the contours vanish into an apparently random jumble of black squiggles, denoting very steep ground. In such places it is essential to have the necessary skills in picking a way through,

Above
From Groban Towards Fisherfield
On Groban, Watershed walkers must look briefly at Fisherfield splendour, before turning east towards The Fannichs.
Ewan Lyons,
Geograph protocol
NH100708

Left
Ben More Assynt from Conival
Naked rock is bright in the afternoon light on Breabag, with the steep crag wall on Ben More Assynt ridge beyond.
Rob Beaumont
NC293180

Meall a Chleirich from Sail Garbh

Sparse vegetation on Meall a Chleirich and her many neighbours looks inviting from equaly rock-marked Sail Garbh.
Nick McLaren
NC405347

round and over slab and crag. Good judgement, confidence and walking poles are the best aids in such demanding terrain, and so it is for some 33km from An Eag all the way to Sgurr Thionail.

There are not enough superlatives in the English language to describe adequately and sufficiently this superb area. The Watershed doesn't exist in isolation from all that surrounds it, of course, with Glen Dessarry, Loch Nevis, a hint of Knoydart, Barrisdale, fiord-like Loch Hourn, and a view of that great sweep of glen and mountain ranged across to the entire south side of south Glenshiel ridge, to complete the scenario. In all of this, the profile of every mountain and succession of tops is ragged. It is no wonder that much of this area is one of the great favourites for so many of those who might be described as being *in a relationship* with wild places. The Watershed weaves a quite magical magnificence in amongst and over this combination of rock, tops, steep passes, and sheer splendour.

South Shiel and Kintail

Munroists love South Glenshiel ridge for the number of ticking-offs that can be achieved in just one outing, but there is far more to it than just that hurried roll call. Approaching from the south and rounding the head of Wester Glen Quoich, by way of the Bealach Duibh Leac, gives an unparalleled lead-in, although perhaps 'lead-on' would be a more fitting description of this part of the journey. It seems as if every top is paraded there in sharp outline, of jagged rock, outcrop, and pinnacle. Once on the ridge, yet another new panorama is unveiled, with Kintail and the Five Sisters drawing the eye down to the tidal waters of Loch Duich. The alternative view to the east is equally grand, with Loch Cluanie tightly hemmed in by crag and shoulder.

Across Glen Shiel, the target is Sgurr a Bhealaich Dheirg, but getting there involves a 600m drop to cross the A87 road to Skye, followed immediately by a 750m climb back out of this deep trench. Boswell and Johnston certainly didn't climb these mountains as they journeyed through by coach, but they did have a good discussion about the shape of a '*protuberance*' further down the Glen. Another mammoth glen-crossing follows with the drop into Fionnglean, the *white glen*, and the equally rapid ascent to Benn Attow, the *long mountain*. Long it is too, with the summit some two kilometres in length, deeply cut on the north-facing side by a series of dramatic corries, separated from each other by narrow sharp ridges, with one of these being the Watershed.

Killilan and West Monar

Size and scale now become distorted by big numbers and distance, by remoteness on an almost unprecedented intensity. For the next section of this magnificent Moine March takes the traveller on a wander through a vast 1,500 square kilometres tract of roadless terrain. Around 40km have a truly cut-off feel, where solitude, and a deep personal interaction with Nature's finest is certain. This should be an unhurried enjoyment, because it promises a unique experience, with the goal being no more than the next hill or lochan. Switch off from the outside world, and tune in to this enfolding splendour.

It is of course not devoid of human impact. Lack of trees is the first and most obvious evidence of this, in an area that is managed in order to maintain deer numbers for the precious stalking season. Some of the lochs which cautiously venture towards the

Beinn Dearg
Morning sun illuminates the
rocks and underside of a snow-
cornice atop the crags on
Beinn Dearg.
Chris Townsend
NH259811

heart of this wildness are man-made, and at the upper reaches of the hydro schemes. The remains of a very long rusting fence, is the legacy of one Colonel Winans's Victorian vanity, and there is the endearing tradition of illicit whisky-making in these remote glens, as far as possible from the prying Excise Man. The occasional cairn and the odd lonely track have but a passing impact on the vast emptiness.

Moruisg and the Moine Mhor

Arriving on Moruisg with its twin tops sets the scene for a different landscape, much of it almost as wild as that which has

Above Left

Loch a Bhealaich and Sgurr Gaorsaic

The view north from Ben Attow is into a vast roadless emptiness where remote glen-heads jostle yet remoter summits.

Jim Shedden
NH012214

Above Right

The Caledonian Canal at Laggan

A yacht motors easily across 'the summit' of the Caledonian Canal at Laggan, fringed with mature woodland.

Peter Wright
NN294976

Left

Sgurr Mor

All is mirrored to perfection, in a festival of rock and crag-crisp ridges radiating from the summit of Sgurr Mor Fannaich.

Richard Kermode, copyright
NH204718

just been traversed. There is, however, rather more evidence of human activity, with a railway and two main roads, which cross the Watershed.

Following the crossing of the A890, the Moine March takes a big loop round the Moine Mhor, which in this case means the *big bog* – why any one of these many bogs should be singled out as being larger than any other is a bit of a mystery, but these names and the descriptions that they convey were of course very local in origin. The going is in places wet underfoot!

Following the descent from Bidein Clann Raonaild to the A832 crossing, an exceptionally fine view down Glen Docherty to

Kinlochewe and Loch Maree, is well worth appreciating. Slioch can just be seen to the right of this superb vista. While to the right of the route, Loch a Croisg, *loch of the crossing* is framed tightly by its flanking hill slopes, and points invitingly towards Achnasheen.

With Fionn Bheinn as the next main objective, there are a couple of hills to be negotiated en route. From the summit of Fionn Bheinn, yet another new world opens up. Loch Fannich

South Glen Shiel from The Five Sisters

The north side of South Glen Shiel Ridge, here viewed from the Five Sisters, is deeply cut by ice-scooped corries.

James Wright
NG976158

Below

Beinn Dronaig and Loch Calavie

Remote Beinn Dronaig stands guard over Loch Calavie, with the Watershed on the rim at the far end of the loch.

Peter Wright
NH059386

Sgur nan Clach Geala

The Fannichs' ridge-horseshoe from Sgurr nan Each to Sgurr Mor round Coire Mor is one of the most rewarding of walks.
Mike Watson, UKC protocol

Below

From Lorguill to Loch Broom

Lorguill is an easy climb, and will repay the effort many times over, with beguiling views in every direction.
Colin Meek
NH238815

provides a level base for the first view of that popular and very appealing group of hills, The Fannichs. They are of course, on the route, but there is a deviation to be made prior to that. The panorama to the west is stunning, with the untamed expanse of Fisherfield and An Teallach to the north-west. The splendour of Torridon lies almost 30km to the west, with the possibility of light catching on The Minch beyond, while there is the promise of perhaps a first glimpse of salt water over 40km to the east, in the inner reaches of the Moray Firth. Some great buttresses of The Fannichs point assertively this way, and certainly serve to reinforce this mountain group's grandeur.

Fannich

Yet again, the Watershed demonstrates that it is no hurry to get to its destination, as it swings once more, first north-east by way of Toll Beag, *little hole*, to within a stone's throw of Loch Fannich, then sharply west up the long ridge of Beinn na Ramh, *hill of the oar* to An Carnan, *the cockroach*. A further westward and wide detour to Groban finally permits access eastwards to this beguiling group of mountains, The Fannichs, where each high point and turning

Ice Climbing in Penguin Gully

The north-facing crags of Beinn Dearg are a winter climber's favourite, here Kenneth Wright ascends Penguin Gully.

Jim deBank
NH252819

Mullach an Leathaid Riabhaich to Loch Glencoul

Rugged splendour of Mullach an Leathaid Riabhaich is a fine match for seaward rock-edged views to Loch Glencoul.

Nick McLaren
NC288247

in this rock-raggled big dipper, provides a new vista. Yes, there is the chance to look back, and reflect on what has been experienced. Indeed, every climber should indulge in this rewarding dalliance – regularly, for it is not just the journey *to* a destination which enriches, but the *entire* experience. There are plenty of fine boulders to sit awhile upon for this reflection, on Sgurr Mor.

When it is time to look to the journey ahead, the panorama is spectacular, and centre stage in this drama is Beinn Dearg. A minor meander round the east end of Loch Droma on the A835 is followed by a modest ridge walk, some of it on one of those strange things, a path, to Beinn Enaiglair. This is a great prominence from which to look down to Loch Broom with the road to Ullapool, and perhaps catch a glimpse of the ferry that is Stornoway-bound.

Dearg Bhraigh

From neighbouring Lorguill, an easy stroll brings the traveller to a formidable dry stane dyke running right across the skyline, and to the right, up onto Beinn Dearg. It is a wonder of that special craft, and has been built solidly on what often looks just like a loose jumble of boulders. A steep crag drops several hundred metres

**From Fionn Bheinn
Towards Ben Wyvis**

Sun finally penetrates the
north-facing corrie on Fionn
Bheinn, with Loch Fannich and
Ben Wyvis in the distance.
Marie Lainton
NH147621

Beinn Leoid
The Watershed journey to
Beinn Leoid from the south is
demanding, but the final push
being easy and rewarding.
Nick McLaren
NC319294

on the north side of it. Although this dyke is a very useful aid to
navigation in poor visibility, it should be noted that it does not go
to the top of the mountain, but veers north about half a kilometre
short of the summit, which is boldly marked with yet another
impressive cairn.

The route takes the Watershed north over a series of great hills,
their ridges randomly littered with lichen-marked boulders, and
lines of craigs cut into their flanks at obscure angles, creating a
route that is anything but direct. To the left, Gleann na Sguaib
and Inverlael, framing that eye catching view towards the Summer
Isles, while to the right, what starts as Gleann Beag, later evolves
into the much larger Gleann Mor, with the road to Strath Carron
and Ardgay. The final flourish in this chain of hills is Seana
Bhraigh. With a long gently rounded summit, and two tops, it
is deeply sculpted to the north with the spectacular Loch Luchd
Choire, and to the right of that Creag an Duine *the precipice of the*

landlord. Beyond, in the treeless Freevatter Forest lies the appealing Strath Mulzie. While to the south is the Cadha Dearg, *red pass*, and the Coire Mor, *big corrie* to the east. Every single hill and mountain tells a visual story, even if it has not come down to us in the form of tradition, we can discover at least some of its saga by looking at the shape and meaning of the hill name. It is a rich tapestry, and one which, alas, the singularly focussed Munro bagger may miss.

A curving arc of ridge then carries the descent east and north to Meall nam Bradham. This provides fine views over Rhidorroch to the north, and beyond that, to the Cromalt Hills. Rhidorroch is a strange and mysterious landscape, with an extensive random

scattering of lochans, and with no apparent pattern to the contours. Relatively low lying at between 200 and 550m, it slopes gently to the north. Interpreting the map in order to discover the location of the Watershed, amongst the jumble of little hills, heather clad moor and those watery areas is a rewarding challenge.

Rhidorroch Cromalt

The transition from Rhidorroch to the Cromalt Hills is at another Loch a Croisge, *loch of the crossing*, Rappach, *the noisy place*, and the first of the hills Meall a Bhuirich Rapaig, is *hill of the bellowing stags*. Clearly it was a place of some significance to our ancestors, and the names that were recorded by the original OS surveyors have stuck. The Moine March in fact just skirts the eastern edge of the Cromalt Hills, but it is a great vantage point from which to look west to Coigach and Cul Mor in Inverpolly. Knockan Crag is but a short distance to the north-west, so the Moine Thrust is here, very close to our route

Conival

The problem with trees again becomes evident and pressing, in the struggle to reach the A837 crossing at about the milestone.

Ben Hee
Mountain and mist combine to create a special attmosphere upon the snow swept rock slopes of Ben Hee.
Mike Watson
NC426339

The plantation before the road presents a formidable battle with pine needle armed branches. Cnoc Chaornaidh with its Chambered Cairns and trig point is on open ground, but getting to spot height 357 through yet more forest is tiresome – this is the polite version!

Breabag beckons and this is achieved by Ruighe Chnoc, Meall a Bhraghaid and Meall Diamhain. With a summit which is over two kilometres long, and a surface landscape character that stands alone on the entire Watershed, Breabag is special. Almost devoid of vegetation, it is an immense jumble of slabs and rocks, which glow almost white in the afternoon sun. Picking a route over and round these boulders, some the size of a large van, is a challenge. Each footfall must be a measured one, in order to attempt to predict the steadiness or otherwise, of each rock. Climbing from the shallow bealach up the south elevation of Conival is a memorable ascent, and one of the few such truly challenging ones on the entire Watershed, where it is certainly much better going up than down. The reward for this vertigo-exposing effort is however breathtaking, for the whole summit is white quartz – a special place.

From Ben Hee to Crask
A random jumble of rock slabs on the summit of Ben Hee give an eye catching foil to the Flows and Ben Klibreck.
Nick McLaren
NC426339

The views west are dramatic, across Inchnadamph and Assynt towards Lochinver. Those iconic mountains of Suilven, Canisp and Quinag (the latter being a property of the John Muir Trust) rear up out of the surrounding lochan-sprinkled moorland, with their respective shapes instantly recognisable. To the east, the mass of Ben More Assynt is linked to this Conival by a narrow ridge. In this area the effects of the Moine Thrust are all around and would most certainly merit further investigation, but at some other time perhaps.

The descent from Conival northwards is initially on a narrow scree-lined ridge, which levels to a gentler slope as it heads for south eastern end of Beinn Uidhe. There, the route descends steeply, calling for extreme care, and then takes the Moine March into a bizarre landscape in which the way is obstructed with a number of steep-flanked ridges running right across the desired route. To get to Beinn Leoid is far from straightforward. The trail then turns sharply to the right from the summit, to take in a succession of modest tops in order to get to Creag an Sgamhlain, overlooking the Lochs More to the left and Merkland to the right. Here is a fine vantage point to admire and contemplate that final rocky flourish on the Moine March, in a horseshoe loop on hills that almost encircles A Glaise.

North West Loop

Following the Lairg to Laxford Bridge (A838) road crossing, some careful route picking is called for, to skirt the assorted lochs and burns, which appear to nudge the Watershed this way and that. Avoiding what are clearly very boggy areas may well prove necessary.

Cairn Dearg is the first goal, and it is noteworthy as the most north-westerly point on the entire Watershed; Cape Wrath is only about 35km from this point. The route, however, swings sharply east and then south to Carn an Tionail, Beinn Direach and Meall a Chleirich, before a rapid descent to the Gobernuisgach track crossing and an equally heart-pumping climb on Sail Garbh. This section skirts the rim of an awe-inspiring 400m deep slab of almost sheer ragged crag, with the higher of the two marked tops

Summit of Ben Attow
The long wide summit of Ben Attow is deeply cut on its north face, with ice-sculpted corries and sharp crisp ridges.
Jim Shedden
NH000196

appearing to teeter on the brink. A final one kilometre approach to the summit of Ben Hee is not especially steep, but the rock-strewn, or perhaps it should it be *rock-obstructed*, terrain gives a vivid impression of how the glacial action during the last Ice Age tore at the surface and then left the job half done, or so it would seem.

As you crest the summit of the mountain the great curtain drops once more, to reveal the full panorama. The cairn, which had been the goal, is eclipsed by the spectrum of all that lies around and ahead.

The Moine March will surely have exceeded all expectation, on a 345km linear trail that is simply spectacular. The familiar theme of variety and diversity holds so very true, whether it be the terrain underfoot, the landscape character, or the much wider panoramic experience, in an endless and ever-changing kaleidoscope of rock, water and sky. The entire March has been a forceful reminder of Nature's all-powerful part in creating this geographic feature, that is now ours to enjoy to the full. The traveller may well have experienced days of perfect solitude, and no matter what the weather may have imposed, the peace will have been Nature's very own.

Peter Wright

Peter Wright

Forsinard Pools

Conservation of RSPB's
Forsinard Flows, with
development of public access
and information is to be
commended.

Norrie Russel, RSPB Forsinard
NC881439

Chapter Six

The Northlands March — *Across the Flows Under the Arc of the Wide Sky*

*I care to live only to entice people
to look at Nature's loveliness.* JOHN MUIR

What is now referred to as 'The Flow Country' has, within the last 30 years or so, gained a special place among our National conservation priorities. This lower lying area in the northern parts of Sutherland and Caithness which may have been dismissed by some, as low status *bog land*, is now appreciated, valued and ranked, not just here in Scotland, but within Europe and the World wide. This kind of peat bog land is rare indeed, and provides a unique habitat rich in biodiversity. The plant, animal and bird species that thrive collectively on it are immensely varied. Why the need, therefore, to make this point so forcibly?

During the 1980s, much of this area in the far north was under threat. Indeed, it was being systematically destroyed, as a

Crask Inn to Ben Hee
So close to the Watershed, the Crask Inn also sits beside the River Tirry, and Ben Hee crowns the western sky-line.
Nick McLaren
NC524245

Badinloskin Ruin

A sad rickle of stones on the moor is all that remains of Badinloskin, where murder was commited in The Clearances.

Nick McLaren

NC722382

Watershed Pools at Loch Bhraigh
From directly above the Watershed at Cnoc Loch Mhadaidh, these pools provide a pleasing foreground for Morven.
Norrie Russel, RSPB Forsinard
NC998318

direct result of an ill-conceived fiscal regime that encouraged the wealthy from elsewhere, to gain a lucrative tax break by buying up and planting thousands of acres of this landscape, with non-native tree species in commercial forestry development. Environmentally this was crass, and morally it was inept: tax avoidance for the rich, and PAYE for the rest of us! It is impossible to write about this area without bringing this comparatively recent situation into the picture, for it has adversely altered the ecosystem on this significant part of the Watershed. The response to this ecosystem destruction was however to bring some key environmental organisations onto the scene, in a way that is making a significant difference in habitat restoration and conservation. This is in turn, enhancing the potential for our enjoyment of the area – for its unique landscape and wildlife qualities.

Here, the Northlands March weaves a 190km route right across the middle of The Flow Country, from Ben Hee in the north-west to Duncansby Head at the north-eastern tip of the Scottish mainland.

Ben Hee, that last really rocky event on the Watershed, other than the coastal experience much further on, is unquestionably one of those hills that are best appreciated by climbing up one side, and down the other. An obvious statement perhaps, but it illustrates so well one of the special qualities of the *way of the Watershed* – a linear route that takes the traveller through

Munsary Dubh Lochans
Plantlife's reserve at Munsary shown from the air, is a fine demontration of the special character of The Flows.
Norrie Russel, RSPB Forsinard
ND217463

highly varied terrain for a specific reason, on a journey with an outstanding purpose. The final push to the summit traverses a scatter of rocks that protrude from the surface at every conceivable angle. Any hope of getting a rhythm to walking uphill is interrupted by this crazy slab terrain. It is invigorating and certainly builds anticipation.

This fine hill not only marks that transition from rock to flow, but is also part of a change in direction for the Watershed.

Creag na h-Iolaire to Ben Klibreck

This is a commanding and rarely seen view of Ben Klibreck over Loch Choire, from the remote Creag na h-Iolaire.

Nick McLaren
NC672288

On leaving the lower of the tops, the route will complete a horseshoe loop that altered it from travelling generally northwards for many hundreds of kilometres, to south, and then eastwards. Ben Hee and her immediate neighbours mark a major turning point on this journey.

Take time then to catch your breath, enjoy the views, identify the neighbouring hills, and marvel especially at those that lie to the north-west. Cape Wrath, which has nothing to do with anger, as the name would suggest, quite simply means the *turning point*, as the north-western tip of Scotland is but 40km away. The upper reaches of all of the mountains that lie between here and there, are almost devoid of vegetation, a landscape entirely dominated by rock. Almost devoid too of track or any habitation, this area's emptiness is majestic. Turn the other way, however, and to the south-east is a distant white dot, just to the right of Ben Klibreck – this may well be the target for the day, the Crask Inn.

Crask

The descent from the higher of the two tops of Ben Hee, to the lower one over a kilometre to the north-east, skirts around the

Stacks of Duncansby
Stacks of Duncansby resplendant in afternoon sun, with Duncansby Head, Pentland Skerries, and Orkney beyond.
Colin Gregory,
Thurso Camera Club
ND397715

rim of the 250m deep chasm of the Allt a Ghorm-choire; this is
the mirror of the earlier experience – though down rather than up.
It still takes your breath away, and acts as yet another reminder
of Nature's splendour. This is followed by an even greater 450m
drop to the head of Loch a Choire Leacaich – an equally breath-
taking experience, which is not for the faint hearted. Ahead, lies
28km of flow, moor and hill, to Creag Sgoilteach, *the hill of the
parting*.

Two more hills with heart-racing ascent and descent complete
the departure from the rocky loop and deposit the route onto real
Flow Country, across a 5km stretch of which there is as much
open water as there is (apparently) firmer ground. Do not be
deceived, however, because much of it is anything but firm. A lot
of careful route-picking and bog-hopping will be called for. Pause
briefly at the trig point on the Cnoc an Alaskie – not only is it only
vaguely a 'cnoc', or *knowe*, but the trig point itself seems to be
sinking into the surrounding peat hag. This is a timely reminder

**From Cnoc Sgriodain
over Vagastie**
From Cnoc Sgriodain on the
shoulder of Ben Klibreck,
Vagastie, Ben Hee, Arkle and
Foinaven, all in evening light.
Nick McLaren
NC549270

though, that all this surrounding peat land is no ordinary bog, but now has high ecological status and is of international importance.

A night in the Crask Inn, which no traveller this way should miss, will provide an opportunity to get dried out and well fed, with the appealing promise of convivial company.

The Crask Inn is only a kilometre from the Watershed here on the Northlands March. Farming and innkeeping are combined, while the absence of mains electricity gives it a basic, yet homely, comfortable charm. It manifests a stunning location facing across the Flow to a skyline which boasts Ben More Assynt and all of the hills around rock-strewn Ben Hee. It sits alone, on that road that goes up the middle of this part of Scotland, from Lairg to Tongue, and has Ben Klibreck almost in its backyard. To visit in the Autumn is to find this remarkable place surrounded by moors which are rich in every hue of yellow, orange, red, crimson and brown. They radiate the passion of the season.

The route then takes a loop onto the shoulder of Ben Klibreck before swinging sharply south across the Bealach Easach, *pass of the horse* to finish this section on Creag Sgoiltech.

Armine

This location then brings the route into a subtly different landscape form for the next 27km to Badinloskin. The so-called

Palm Loch
Sunny Palm Loch beside the lonely Syre to Kinbrace road, with Beinn a Mhadaidh in shadow, and Ben Griam Beg.
Peter Wright
NC706410

Loch of Lomashion

Loch of Lomashion is attractive
to bird life, judging by the
ribbon of lush vegetation
around it's moorland margins.
Peter Wright
ND386699

Ben Armine Forest, is a misnomer, for like so many erstwhile 'forests' it is almost entirely treeless, and the word has been commandeered for the general description of 'deer forest': no shortage of this four-legged species hereabouts. It is however, a mix of moor, small areas of Flow, and nestles within a huge amphitheatre seemingly surrounded by hills. It is drained by the Black Water flowing to the south east. In the middle of this secret enclosed world lies the Ben Armine Stables bothy, where the door is always open, where there is the delightful novelty of sleeping platforms cleverly constructed between the former pony stalls, and the pleasure of warming yourself by a peat fire. The peat spade is provided so that you can do the right thing and replenish the peat stack at the gable end before you resume the journey.

The exit is by way of Creag na h-Iolaire, with a steep descent to the very flat bottomed valley preceding Truderscaig, with its Loch, plethora of ancient hut circles, and a very out of place commercial forest. This is best skirted to get to Cnoc na Gaothe which sits proudly beside Loch Rimsdale, a shallow sheet of water directly connected to Loch Nan Clar, and in turn connected to Loch Badanloch; three lochs in one. Two kilometres to the north and almost exactly on the Watershed are the sad ruins of Badinloskin, where one of the worst atrocities of the Sutherland estate

Creag na h-Iolaire
Calm on Loch Nan Clar, with exquisite shafts of sunlight on rain, between Creag na h-Iolaire and Ben Klibreck.
Peter Wright
NC672228

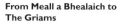

From Meall a Bhealaich to The Griams

From Meall a Bhealaich, lochans, Meall a Mhuirich and Ben Griam Beg, with flowing and overlapping hill-lines.

Colin Gregory,
Thurso Camera Club
NC893404

Below
Cnoc Riabhach

Pylons being adapted for renewable marine energy march between Meall a Beallaich and Cnoc nam Bo Riabhaich.

Colin Gregory,
Thurso Camera Club
NC919377

clearances occurred. Patrick Sellar, the Duke of Sutherland's henchman set fire to this house while a bed-ridden 90-year-old lady was confined within. She was rescued by what was left of the local population, but died two days later. Sellar stood trial for murder some time later, but was found not guilty. History has been a more rational judge of the man.

Rosail and Griam Beg

Beinn Rosail provides a brief venture onto slightly higher ground, before a 12km rambling experience through terrain that is neither one thing nor the other. It is not quite Flow, it is not all bog; it has few distinguishing features, and the route seems almost

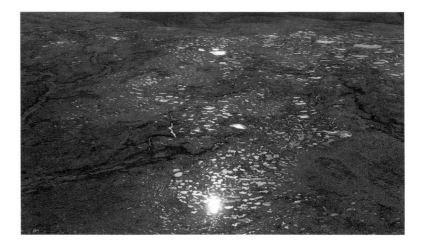

aimless. It is, however, a strangely beautiful landscape beneath the captivating dome of wide sky. The next objective stands bold and brave to the south-east – Ben Griam Beg, with almost 300m of challenging ascent to be conquered to reach a hilltop that is dominated by two features. Firstly, it is the site of an extensive ancient fortification, and secondly, it is the dominant place in the wider landscape. To the north, Strath Halladale stretches long and straight ocean-wards, while Strath Ullie or Strath of Kildonan carries the eye south, before this famous valley then swings east towards the Sea. That recurrent theme of a keen sense of place is so apt here, and vividly places it in its much wider context. This is one of the relatively few locations where two major valleys and their respective rivers emanate from the same bog on the Watershed. The eastern side of this valley genesis is presided over by Meall a Bhealaich, *hill of the pass*, with its visually intrusive communication mast.

Knockfin

Knockfin Heights await the traveller, and the name at least gives a somewhat misleading impression of what can be expected, it is a paradox, because the word heights might imply something reasonably solid. This area is one of the finest of its kind in the entire Flow Country, and the Northlands March goes right across the middle of it. Open water abounds, and it takes some skill

in reading the terrain to ascertain what parts of the vegetation surrounding this, is possible, never mind safe, to walk on. On a bright sunny day with a light breeze, though there is little to match this place. With adrenalin racing as you bog-hoppingly venture to cross it dry-shod, the dancing light on all of the pools, the wide palette of colour in the sphagnum mosses and moor grass, and the wide vistas to Morven and her shapely neighbours to the south-east, the scene is beguiling.

A strangely named shooting lodge to the north, The Glut, lies in a hill-girt hollow. The onward journey is however north-eastward to Ben Alisky and its near neighbour of exactly the same height, Beinn Glass-choire. Where else on the Watershed have we encountered another Coire Ghlais?

Alisky and Stemster

There follows a 15km stretch which though lacking any major features, is dotted with the occasional *dubh lochan*, and the delight of the contrasting dancing light that these exhibit. The two trig

Clifftop
Pentland Skerries seemingly within touching distance, between the cliffs of a geo and across the Firth.
Colin Gregory,
Thurso Camera Club
ND401733

Below
Sordale Hill Cottage Ruin
In the general retreat from the Watershed, this cottage on Sordale Hill has been abandoned to the forces of Nature.
Colin Gregory,
Thurso Camera Club
ND157619

points show, if nothing else does, that the Ordnance Survey did not neglect the area in its survey programme over a hundred and fifty years ago. Crossing the A9 is a strange if brief encounter with tarmac, after so much absolutely trackless terrain. There follows a final and short sweep south by Crofts of Benachielt and then directly north to Sheppardstown. If the weather is clear, the Fraserburgh coast can be seen far to the south-east, beyond the outer reaches of the Moray Firth and the shapely Mormond Hill stands to the south of this.

The gentle slopes of Stemster Hill, and its loch of the same name, herald a major change in direction. A challenging 15km trek north through a landscape that is low on the scale of any attractive features, is marred by a line of pylons, sullied by commercial forest and not very well concealed electricity sub-

The stones of the ancient cairn on Warth Hill provide a modest viewpoint for Firth, Skerries and indeed, to Orkney.

Colin Gregory,
Thurso Camera Club
ND371598

station, and finally, dominated by a big wind farm. After this environmental confusion, the wild flowers on Spittal Hill are a welcome sight.

Bower and Slickly

The River Thurso to the left, which is somewhat blighted by that wind farm, heralds the town of Thurso on the Atlantic coast. Sheltered in its bay, it is of course one of the main ferry ports for Orkney, and was developed as a planned town on the former prosperity of flagstone quarrying in the area. With another few kilometres northwards to Sordale Hill, the route then swings sharply east across rough grazing and patches of bog to Mounthalie and its enticing views of the pink western cliffs of the island of Hoy. The landscape then becomes leg-testingly rougher across tussock moorland, with blocks of commercial forest to be negotiated, and with the distant communication mast at Brabster, by way of the quaintly named Hill of Slickly, as the next target.

The Stacks

More low lying moorland peppered with a number of water lily lochans takes the route east and leaves the Atlantic views behind, for on Warth Hill the North Sea coastline is but a short distance ahead. The A99 road to John O' Groats presents the brief and last tarmac-crossing on the Scottish mainland, and is quickly followed by a final spread of trackless moorland, from where the conclusion of the Northland March can be both seen and eagerly anticipated.

The Pentland Firth
Tide and wave power. Stroma and the hills of Hoy from Duncansby Head – north-eastern tip of the UK mainland.
Colin Gregory,
Thurso Camera Club
ND402236

Loch of Lomashion harbours rich birdlife, and its margins are rough, yet lush with the guano that they have left. The noisy cliff top is reached immediately to the north of Fast Geo, and the final four kilometres of this, the Northland March, are along the precarious cliff edge. Stacks of Duncansby stand defiant and proud against the constant action of waves, and provide a guard of honour for the traveller towards Duncansby Head. There, the lighthouse is the marker for journey's end on the mainland of Scotland. However, a tantalising sight across the Pentland Firth points to the possibility of the Watershed extending further north, by Pentland Skerries, through the Orkney and Shetland Islands.

Were we able to wind the clock back a mere 11,000 years we would find that this would not in fact be journey's end, for until around that time, Orkney was a peninsula, and not a detached archipelago of Islands as we see it today. Yet, further back into the mists of time, the same would be said of what we now call Fair Isle and the Shetland Islands, but the entire land-form of northern Europe was then very different, with a rather smaller North Sea, filling only its contemporary northern reaches.

Where better to reflect upon the many qualities of the Northlands March, than here at Duncansby Head? Author Neil Gunn, who wrote so evocatively of his beloved Caithness, said:

This is the northland, land of exquisite light.

We would be hard pressed to improve on that very succinct
evocation of all that it meant to him. We can draw on this
inspiration, and discover for ourselves the subtle and immensely
beautiful character of the area. The Flow Country and her bio-rich
boglands have been a discovery and a delight. The bold outcrops
that afford such magnificent views across and down valley and
moor, the full spectrum of season-evolving colours, the coastline
and the vistas beyond, and the knowledge that more of this
landscape is now designated and protected, than anywhere else
on this scale on the entire Watershed, have all focussed the mind
and heart on a simply spectacular experience. The *old bogland* has
emerged as something to celebrate, and a place to take time to
appreciate fully.

Long stretches of the route are quite uninhabited, and
demonstrate, *par excellence*, the notion that countryside that is no
good for agriculture is perfect for wildlife. The two voluntary
sector environmental organisations that are doing most to foster,
protect and widen the appeal of the area are Plantlife and the Royal
Society for the Protection of Birds (RSPB), with the latter now
generating very significant public support for what it is doing, on
an ever widening area.

Neil Gunn's simple evocation echoes down the years to us
today, to gladden the spirit.

Jim Shedden

Peter Wright

Fair Isle

Remote Fair Isle, midway
between the Orkney
and Sheltand Islands is a
great favourite for keen
ornithologists.

NTS photo library

HZ207751

Opposite

**Pentland Firth from
The Wing**

Aptly named The Wing, this
tip of South Ronaldsay is a fine
place to ponder the Pentland
Firth and to the UK Mainland.

Fiona Isbister

ND437837

Chapter Seven   The Viking March – *Between Ocean and Sea*

This sudden splash into pure wildness –
baptism in Nature's warm heart –
how utterly happy it made us.
Nature streaming into us, wooing,
 teaching her wonderful glowing lessons . . . JOHN MUIR

Bringing the two great archipelagos of Orkney and Shetland into the Watershed story is entirely fitting. So often tagged on to the map of Scotland, appearing misplaced somewhere in the North Sea, belies their true place, especially in this epic story. They form a central part in the geographic saga.

The route that has been plotted here is based primarily on identifying the shallowest passage between islands. In other words, were sea levels to drop, at what points the islands would re-connect? Sea charts provided the information necessary to achieve this fascinating exercise. For what we see today, are apparently disconnected islands, with firths, sounds and open water, separating one from the other, but which in the wider

From Keelylang Hill to Scapa Flow

Wisps of cloud drift slowly over the moors of Keelylang Hill, with Scapa Flow backed by the hills of Hoy.

*Hannah Longmuir,
Borders Exploration Group*
HY377102

timeline of geographic evolution, have only comparatively recently become detached. Wind the clock back just some 11,000 years, and what you would find would be the Orkney Peninsula. Travel yet further back in time, and the Shetland Islands would similarly be peninsular. Although within these timespans many other changes to our landscapes have occurred, one constant has been this geographic feature – the Watershed.

Thanks to the detail on those sea charts, a route can be drawn with some confidence, as it sweeps across from island to island. To walk the landward parts of such a route would be immensely challenging, for it is entirely where Nature put it, and does not bear any relation whatever to practicalities like public ferry services. That, however, is the way of the Watershed, and to make that journey in spite of the logistics of inter-island travel would be a supreme pleasure.

A direct link between Duncansby Head and South Ronaldsay, by way of Pentland Skerries, would be challenging indeed, with the problems of vertical cliffs and rapid tides to be overcome. Much better and safer then, to be content with a photograph or two from the headland, enjoy a short ferry ride from John O' Groats to Burwick, and then a short walk to Brough Ness on the southern tip of the island.

Rousay From Looma Shun
Island dreaming in a soft light, from Looma Shun to Rousay, Wyre, Egilsay, and perhaps to Eday – on the journey.
Fiona Isbister
HY359237

By Barriers and Beyond

Much of South Ronaldsay is worked farmland, with a mix of permanent grazing and some arable; there are only a few areas which are truly wild. This pattern of use however, provides a good habitat for wild flowers and all of the abundant wildlife that these attract. With the seashore never very far away, the mix of birdlife is varied too. There are, however, a large number of fences and dykes to be negotiated in this part of the island, and fields full of cattle, that are nothing, if not curious. Frequent detours may therefore be necessary. After the crossings by Burray, the Holms and the Churchill Barriers, Orkney mainland is reached just east of St Mary's.

Highland Park Distillery on the outskirts of Kirkwall is the next target, and a cause for delay perhaps, before turning west by the Youth Hostel, and leaving this brief brush with urban settlement behind. Wideford Hill crowned with its untidy clutter of masts and associated buildings beckons, with a succession of minor roads and fences to be crossed en route. Ignoring all the trappings

Eyenhallow Sound

Twice daily since the very
advent of time, tides have
flowed between ocean and sea,
around Eyenhallow, Orkney.

Fiona Isbister

HY335288

North Ronaldsay

On North Ronaldsay,
the shoreline and rocks are
ever-close, and the gesture of
the waves captivating.

John Tulloch,
North Ronaldsay Trust
HY781570

of modern communication infrastructure, the view from atop Wideford is a delight, and will provide good cause for a pause to fully appreciate the panoramic round.

Dropping down to the north, Burrey Brae is the next goal,

Egilsay
The tide has ebbed on Egilsay,
and left the white sand,
rock and seaweeds for us
to appreciate.
Jen Trendall
HY479301

Eday
Texture of sky and moor,
rock and light mingle delightfully
here on Eday, near the Stone
of Setter.
Hayley Warriner
HY564374

Nesting with Sand Water Loch

Shetland landscape worth protecting – nesting with Sand Water Loch looking north-east from Hill of Skurron.

Frank Hay,
Viking wind farm Campaign
HU410576

followed by a swing west to Keelylang Hill and a succession of modest heather-clad moorland hills, and heading for spot 37 on the A965. The wetlands just to the west of Loch of Wasdale may prove challenging, but firmer ground is reached on the ascent to Burrien Hill. The route then follows a wide ark on the gently undulating higher ground, over rough heather and peat banks, with eye catching and ever changing views as a compelling distraction from the journey itself. A brief dalliance at the wind farm on Burgar Hill, or in the viewing hides overlooking Lowrie's Water, are quickly followed by the descent to Point of Hisber where the power of flood tides on Eynhallow Sound cannot fail to impress.

Island Hopping

Eynhallow requires special arrangements with a local boatman, but a visit would fully repay the effort, for it is a special place. On Rousay, it will be hard not to be enticed away briefly from the journey, by the historical remains at Mid Howe and Westside,

but the range of hills from Mansemass Hill to Kierfea Hill by way of Twelve Hours Tower do require your attention if you are to proceed. Yet again, the elevated position provides views to all points of the compass that are a joy to behold. A short loop by Faraclett then brings the Watershed down to the shore for a crossing to Holm of Scockness. The visit to Egilsay will be brief,

Muckle Flugga
Sea mist around Muckle Flugga rock and lighthouse – only tiny Out Stack somewhere beyond in the Norwegian Sea.
Mike Pennington, copyright
HP609183

Below
Italian Chapel
Faith and creative genius enabled Italian POW's to convert this wartime Nissen Hut into a Renaisance chapel.
Fiona Isbister
HY488006

but immensely worthwhile, for in addition to the ruins of the church where Magnus Erlendsson (St Magnus) was murdered in about 1117, the wild flowers will in season, be exquisite.

Landfall on Eday is at Seal Skerry from where the Watershed then heads for Flaughton Hill before moving north by Stennie Hill, and leaves the island at Greeny Brae. A two-kilometre crossing to Hegglie Ber on Sanday is followed by a long north-easterly amble by machair, dune and sweet-scented grassland to Fea Hill, and eventually leaving the island at its northern tip of Tofts Ness. North Ronaldsay, the most remote of these Islands is reached at Point of Burrian. With the highest point on the island being a mere 20m above sea level, and never more than 3km from the shore, that special interface between island and sea is intense. The land is fertile, well-farmed, and thanks to the great dyke that surrounds the island, the sheep are kept out on the shore, to thrive on a diet of seaweed. Our final link with Orkney is then severed at Seal Skerry.

Fair Isle

Getting to Fair Isle by public ferries and transport from North Ronaldsay involves a long and circuitous journey. Although it is roughly equidistant from both Seal Skerry and Horse Island off the southern tip of the Shetland Islands, it is necessary to return to Kirkwall, then ferry north to Lerwick on Shetland, followed by a bus journey south to Grutness, and finally on another ferry to North Haven.

Unst – North Water

From Libbers Hill on Unst,
North Water and Heimar
Water catch the sun and lie
gently in the wild landscape.

Mike Pennington,
copyright
HP583133

Loch of Tingwall
Loch of Tingwall with Hill
of Steinswall offer typical
experience of Shetland
ladscape, inviting further
exploration.
Calum Togood
HU416436

Fair Isle is administratively part of the Shetland Islands, but those 37km from The Nizz to Horse Island, West of Sumburgh Head, reinforce its isolation and almost unique character. Owned by the National Trust for Scotland, it has a small but active community in which a combination of independence and active co-operation ensure that it can survive in such a remote location. The population increases throughout the summer months with the influx of bird watchers, and those who come simply to appreciate all that the wild isolation has to offer. The Watershed comes ashore at Head of Tind having touched briefly on the sea stacks of The Skerry and The Keels – another graphic reminder of the interface between land and sea. The route then meanders through the small settlement at the south of the island, before holding close to the West coast by Hoini and Burrashield. Finally, from Ward Hill, it drops steeply to the north-east, and disappears beneath the waves at The Nizz.

The hidden link with the next group of islands is by way of a ridge on the sea bed which is markedly shallower than the waters on either side. At about the half-way, there is a feature marked on the sea chart which is ominously called 'The Hole'.

The final section of this epic, places the route firmly upon the spine of the Shetland Islands, the most northerly part of the entire

UK. This long narrow archipelago appears to reach beyond, to
stretch out as it were, as if to make a deliberate effort to distance
itself from the Scottish mainland. Indeed, there are those living
on Shetland who would gladly secede from the UK altogether, but
that contention is for another forum. Two key factors determine
the line of the Watershed, with the Atlantic Ocean and the North
Sea each pressing their cause against an ever-narrowing divide.
Plotting the shallowest route between islands, from Fair Isle to
Unst, by way of the Shetland mainland and Yell provides the basis
upon which the line is first sketched out, while the encroachment
by a myriad of Sounds and Voes, and the sources of burn and
bog combine to give it some shape. Finally, it is yet again the
higher ground and the hills which articulate the precise line of the
Watershed that we have chosen to follow.

If Shetland seems remote, with a major journey just to get
there, then be prepared to be richly rewarded for the effort. This
Islands trek, will straddle three of the main islands, and two
islets. Carrying a pocket geology guide is a must, for the entire
archipelago is now a UNESCO Geopark, with ample visible
evidence of everything from colliding tectonic plates, volcanoes,
fossils, erratic boulders, lava flows, geo-walls, and so much more.
Fifteen different or overlapping designated areas impact upon

the Watershed, and serve to highlight the value of landscape and habitat. A number of organisations play an active part in maintaining and safeguarding this roll call of environmental excellence, and chief amongst them is the Shetland Amenity Trust.

Shetland Mainland

As the route of the Watershed has taken us ever northwards, so the origins of all of the place names have evolved with that progress. Here on Shetland, it is the Norse influence that predominates. The constant theme of emptiness prevails – well, almost. In the 80km of Watershed on the mainland, there are but three scattered settlements, a handful of houses, and two airfields. Communication masts are in evidence, and both the presence and the threat of wind turbines cannot be ignored. Plenty of wind there may be, but to harness it carries a heavy price in both subsidy and landscape destruction. The trackless nature of the route takes it over rough grassland, moor, marsh, flow, and minor hill, in an ever changing, ever demanding terrain. The sounds of the sea, birdlife and breeze are ever-present, and bring to the traveller an immensely rich diversity of experience.

From Hogg of the Ness just south of Sumburgh Airfield, the

Brough of Bigga on Yell
Waters of Yell Sound from Mio Ness on 'The Mainland', with uninhabited Bigga, and the modest hills of Yell.
Calum Togood
HU424791

mystery borne in an unfamiliar language is intriguing, as feature after feature marks out the journey. Erne's Ward and Ward of Scousburgh are followed by Hallilee, and Royl Field – which is anything but a field. On Sheens of Breitoe some bog-hopping is needed, while Bersa Hill is indeed quite hill-like. The views to both sides of Hill of Steinswall are enlivened by the silvery dancing light on the surface of the Lochs and Voes. Just seven kilometres to the east is Lerwick, the capital of these Shetland Islands. A proud former Royal Burgh, it maintains its cultural traditions, and its tightly packed core of closes and flag-stoned lanes. Modern, contemporary activity maintains a busy harbour which still services fishing, inter-island transport, and that economic mainstay, the oil industry. This brief brush with urban activity, soon gives way however to more moor and mire by Hill of Hamarsland and Hill of Mid Skurron.

If Nature's pilgrim is being true to this calling, then self-sufficiency and wild camping are essential. So too, is it necessary to be well-organised with food and equipment. The dividend is however, in the eco-rich engagement which this virtue will bring.

The north end of the mainland is a place of contrast. East Kame, South Filla Runnie, and Hill of Susetter, followed by

Lichen on Egilsay

Lichen-sprouting gravestone in the ancient churchyard on Egilsay.

Jen Trendall

HY466304

Souther Hill and Hill of Oxnabool, all have a wild splendour; they give a real feeling of being detached from the everyday. At Hill of Crooksetter this all changes though, with the vast engineering capacity of Sullom Voe Terminal, but a kilometre to the west. Shetland's wealth. Then, just as rapidly, that industrial icon fades into the distance, with the end of the mainland in sight at Croo Taing.

Yell

At somewhat less than 500m wide, Bigga might seem to be a misnomer, but it is a strategic stepping stone to the next, the Island of Yell.

With that quick step to Point of Sheetsbrough, our route lies eastward and then north to Hill of Clothan, where the journey continues through the centre of the island, on terrain that is reminiscent of much of the earlier Flow Country. Often wet underfoot, it calls for that by now well-tested talent for reading the terrain, and working out where best to tread. With a number of protected sites straddling the route, these habitats are clearly of great importance. Beyond Hill of Noub there is an apparently

Cotton Grass on Saxa Vord to Muckle Flugga
Radiant bog cotton heads on Saxa Vord in late evening, looking across Burra Firth to the most northerly of the UK Stacks.
Mike Pennington, copyright HP630176

aimless feel to the pilgrimage as it swings round the heads of conflicting burns, touches upon Kame of Sandwick before turning north again, and dropping down to the A968 crossing at Setter.

This apparent aimlessness continues throughout the North of the island too, and enters a watery landscape spread between Hill of Camb and Knowes of Bratta. Watery, however, holds yet again, all the promise of that silver dancing light on the succession of lochs to both left and right. The west and Atlantic coast beckons briefly, before the journey is drawn east in a loop by Hill of Vigon and Wards of Grimsetter. At Virdi Point, the tantalising sight of the very last island in the chain, the final section of this immense geographic and landscape-rich journey, is almost within touching distance, less than a kilometre across the waters of the Bluemull Sound.

Unst

The name Gallow Hill may have a grim resonance, and is a mere 99m in height, but it is a boldly rocky outcrop which fully repays every carefully chosen step to the summit, with sheer delight. The journey then carries north into the final 18km, which have four overlapping forms of designation and protection as SSSI, SPA, NNR, and NSA; this is no ordinary landscape, no minor bit of countryside. Within this cornucopia of environmental diversity it is hard not to pause frequently to marvel at the surroundings. From Libbers Hill the traveller is once again conscious of the narrow interface between ocean and sea. Those dramatic cliffs to the left bring the Atlantic almost to your feet, or so it seems, while to the right, the Burra Firth cuts a deep and steep mini-fiord, filled with the waters of the North Sea.

On the shapely rounded Hermaness Hill, the immensity of this whole Watershed experience wells up, as a thousand chattering memories jostle for pride of place.

Standing here on the clifftop overlooking the wide horizon that merges beyond, into the Norwegian Sea, contemplating the scene, reflecting and looking back on this very special Scottish journey there is no doubt that it has given in abundance, a fine share of 'the winds that blow their freshness'.

Jim Shedden

Peter Wright

Sgurr Mor

Affectionately known as 'Sgurr Mor Fannaich', to give it a fitting distinction, it reigns supreme within The Fannichs.

Chris Townsend
NH203718

Chapter Eight

Threats and Conservation – *Creating a Legacy from the John Muir Centenary*

One is constantly reminded of the infinite
lavishness and fertility of Nature –
inexhaustible abundance amid what seems
like enormous waste. And yet when we look
into her operations that lie within reach of our minds,
we learn that no particle of her material is wasted or
worn out. It is eternally flowing from use to use,
beauty to yet higher beauty.

What organisational and political avenues can be exploited in order to grasp the key place of the Watershed in our landscapes, and its potential for our cultural life, health and wellbeing? That is the most compelling question that *Nature's Peace* and the call by Muir to '*do something for wildness*' presents. Allied to this is the very simple further issue: of the vision for the Watershed. If we can begin satisfy these compelling challenges, we will have gained an immeasurable benefit and be enormously enriched.

Our ribbon of wildness is a linear geographic feature within the wider landform of Scotland. It has evolved slowly, and generally undergone the least evident human impact – a unique distinction for a feature on this scale. It links so many designated and protected areas, features characteristics which are continuously at the higher end of the Wild Land spectrum, and serves to link sites and the work of every single national environmental organisation. For all these reasons, it merits greater appreciation and protection.

Although you could walk for great distances along the route, and see little or no apparent evidence of human activities, this would be deceptive. You could experience great remoteness and isolation, and fully enjoy all that

Loch Hourn
At the head of Loch Hourn with Barrisdale on the right, the mountains of the Watershed rise rough and steep.
Keith Brame
NG943072

Conival

Conival crowns a geologists
treasure trove, with the
Geopark on the far side
celebrating its special status.
Chris Townsend
NC303199

Culra Bothy

Recently refurbished by the Mountain Bothies Association, Culra Bothy looks resplendant with Ben Alder as neighbour.

Alan Bowie,
Mountain Bothies Association
NN521761

these precious landscape qualities bring; you would readily be wooed by the notion of the largely continuous relative wildness of the Watershed and its surrounding landscapes; but the picture is not as universally intact. Sheep and deer grazing for our purposes, have over hundreds of years, altered the ground cover vegetation, and hence the habitats these support. Fences, dykes, masts, tracks, roads, canal and rail crossings, muir burn, a few houses and just one urban development (on the mainland) have all had some direct visual impact. The wildness, though relative, has in places, been eroded.

The impact of earlier heavy industrial blight in the Laich March has now largely faded from the scene, and indeed, given half a chance, Nature is reclaiming her own. New forms of engineering infrastructure are however sullying the face of this highly visible landscape feature. Wind farms and all of the clutter which they bring, are an intrusion. The proposal for new large scale pump storage hydro power construction hangs like a grim threat over at least one part of the ribbon of wildness. Government targets for substantial forestry expansion cannot but encroach upon the Watershed. Modest but real urban development will forever remove areas of current wilder land.

Bodesbeck Law to Ettrick Pen

The jumbled cairn atop Bodesbeck Fell is a fine vantage, but every match for the full expansive panorama in the round.

Kerry Muirhead,
Ettrick and Yarrow Valleys
NT169104

In the John Muir Trust's Wild Land Campaign, the aim is: 'to highlight the threats to wild land, and to present practical solutions to protecting what remains'.

The relative wildness of land has been vividly illustrated on a map which the JMT produced. This shows a spectrum from the most remote and wildest ten per cent of the countryside as the most precious and meriting much fuller protection, through the various lesser but nonetheless significant shades of wilder land, to the urban built up areas, with low status within this argument. This map provides a very graphic illustration of the place and relative priority of wildness throughout the Scottish landscape. Were the Watershed to be plotted on this map, it would be both generally and consistently at the higher, and indeed, often the highest end of the spectrum.

In a partnership between the Association for the Protection of Rural Scotland and the Scottish Campaign for National Parks, a strong case is argued for the creation of up to seven new National Parks spread widely across our most valued mountain and coastal

Duncansby Head Lighthouse

With Pentland Skerries beyond, Duncansby Head and lighthouse set a dramatic note for this north-east tip of UK mainland.

Colin Grergory, Thurso Camera Club
ND405732

**Head of the River Tweed
from Annanhead Hill**

From around snow shadows
on Flecket Hill, the headwaters
of the mighty River Tweed set
course for the North Sea.

David Lintern
NT061134

areas. Three of these proposed areas would include landscapes on and about the Watershed.

Scottish Natural Heritage has carried out a comprehensive exercise in defining the area of Scotland which best characterise Wildness and Wild Land. It has identified five key factors in its Mapping Scotland's Wildness and Wild Land. These are: relative wildness, ruggedness, perceived naturalness, remoteness from roads and ferries, and absence of man-made artefacts. Again, in tracing the Watershed through the maps for each of these factors, it maintains a profile which, with only minor and brief exceptions, demonstrates higher quality terrain throughout.

The generic working group on the John Muir Centenary Celebration has identified three key objectives which all partners have committed to work towards. These are:

- To increase awareness of and interest in John Muir and the value and importance of Scotland's great outdoors, including its landscapes and wild places.

- To encourage more people to connect with Scotland's outdoors – its nature and landscapes – by experiencing it, exploring it and helping look after it.

A Chaileach

A Chaileach, the old woman, is gatekeeper to The Fannichs from the west and sets the scene to perfection.

Kathryn Goodenough, Geograph protocol
NH135714

- To encourage more people to visit Scotland through its links with John Muir.

Nature's Peace presses all of the buttons within each of these National initiatives and goals.

Nature's Peace is topical, and undoubtedly of our time. It will bring to a growing audience a new appreciation, understanding and enjoyment of a major geographic feature which transcends much of the Scottish landform in a way that is entirely novel. It is an original. The quality of the photographs and the skilled landscape interpretation of the many photographers provide a powerful visual dimension to the case being argued here. Throughout each of the six Marches, the camera has captured images which are both immensely enjoyable to look at and assimilate, and build a strong case.

The inevitable call for the Watershed to become some form of Long Distance Route (LDR) has already been heard, albeit in muffled voice. Thankfully, this is most unlikely to happen, and the saving grace is that it bounds or crosses the territories of 13 different (mainland) local authorities. None of it is currently

Forsinard
The RSPB does a superb job at and around Forsinard in safeguarding and sharing the splendour of The Flows.
Norrie Russel,
RSPB Forsinard
NC868423

designated as LDR, so the planning implications alone would frustrate any such a plan for the foreseeable future. *Nature's Peace* is about a much wider concept.

None of the standard environmental designations including, SSSI, Ramsar Site, Special Protection Area (SPA), National Park, or Special Area of Conservation (SAC), would be worth pursuing, because the Watershed, in spite of its wider qualities, does not as a whole fit the necessary landscape and habitat requirements for these various forms of protection.

With the rapid succession of The Year of Natural Scotland in 2013, and the John Muir Centenary in 2014, there is a prime opportunity to propose a long term vision for the Watershed of Scotland. The powerful combination of the photographs here in *Nature's Peace*, which have been so readily contributed by a significant number of genuinely motivated people and organisations, and the text to expand upon this visual imperative, ensure that there is here the highly appealing start to the case for a vision for the future.

The Vision is: the designation and creation of a chain of UNESCO Biosphere Reserves centred upon the Watershed of Scotland and thus incorporating many of the higher status Wild Land areas referred to earlier.

There could be as many as 15 'Core Areas' along this chain. A rather smaller number of larger 'Buffer Zones' around and in places connecting Core Areas, would anchor the chain to local communities and the people living in them, and to wider river catchments. Finally, the entire chain would be linked along and around the Watershed with one continuous 'Transition Area'.

This vision is nothing if not ambitious, and it is certainly radical in the way in which it would imply that we can make something of a hitherto undreamed of aspiration for our landscapes and people. We can grasp this unique opportunity to do something truly distinctive with the recognition and care of these wilder areas of the country, and critically, the central part that people and communities must play in the whole process. To propose a linked chain of designated area running

Forest Ride

Decaying fencepost provides a rich habitat for mosses and lichens, in this avenue through the monoculture.

Peter Wright
NT533015

the length, along the whole of Scotland, on this one immense geographic feature is unconventional, but pushes the bounds and the possibilities into an entirely new and infinitely worthwhile environmental realm.

It may take a decade or more to achieve this vision, but it is rooted in a single feature that Nature has provided, and will set in motion an exciting new order from which yet more possibilities will most surely emerge.

The author invites all those with an interest in the Watershed, our ribbon of wildness, and in embracing some radical new thinking for Scotland's Natural environment and her people, to give this their serious consideration.

Peter Wright

Sunrise and cloud inversion

Summer dawn cloud-inversion over Assynt, from the hills of Rhidorroch – mystery and promise of a new day.

Peter Wright

Loch Skeen

Tucked into a loop in the
Watershed, Loch Skeen
gathers the waters that then
become the Grey Mare's Tail.

Peter Wright

Rotten Bottom
From this snow-clad Rotten Bottom to Hart Fell, the Watershed crests the rim of a succesion of precipitous crags.
David Lintern

Opposite
Fraoch Bheinn
Fraoch Bheinn sits uncompromisinly astride the Watershed, between the upper reaches of glens Kingie and Dessary.
David Lintern

Chapter Nine   An End that is Just the Beginning ...

The inspiration for this book has, of course, been twofold. Firstly, John Muir to whom we owe an immense debt of gratitude for all that he did for wildness and people in his lifetime, and his written and organisational legacy. Secondly, we are moved by the power of the camera, when combined with the skill of the photographer. The one provides the means to exploit the other. So what better reason, timing and method whereby to celebrate the landscapes of the Watershed of Scotland?

As a man who loved the experiences and all the possibilities in a very long journey, guided only by Nature and his close spiritual interaction with it, John Muir has most surely given us something to which to aspire. In *Nature's Peace* there is a call to wake up and smell the sedges and the earth, hear the sound of the skylark, fill your eyes with colour and ever changing light, be in awe of rock and crag, tread wisely, take in the wonder of the far horizon, feel

the wildness in your soul, let your spirit be uplifted to soar in the caress of this clear air.

    There is something very special in having an in-depth knowledge and sense of intimacy with such a long and continuous swathe of the Scottish landscape. The author can visualise almost every top and bealach, every major bog and area of forest, all the big ascents and descents, and so much more. He can call to mind a significant kaleidoscope of the great panoramas, and recall a multitude of little details experienced along the way. This is of course, so much more than just intimacy and memories however, for the entire journey was one of never ending interaction with the terrain, the landscapes, the weather, and all that Nature both gave and expected. Whether Nature's beating heart was measured in the passing days on the move, or the fine succession of tops, or in the changing seasons, or more vaguely in the ever unfolding vistas, or indeed in every single footfall, that living beating rhythm was vibrant and generous.

Sgurr na Ciche
As the cloud lours just above head height on Sgurr na Ciche, the sun makes a deffiant mark on Morar by Loch Nevis.
Larry Foster

Loch Mhoicean

Remote and captivating Loch Mhoicean is guarded by the Watershed's Meall Shuas and points to An Cruachan.

Peter Wright

To stand anywhere at all upon this ribbon of wildness is to discover a gentle and subtle connection with an eternal creativity and renewal, to tune in to it and be part of it, and engage fully with it is indeed in the spirit of *Nature's Peace*.

As you have looked at the photographs, hopefully been inspired by the beauty of the landscapes and moments that each has captured, and made your own connections, how do they nourish your spirit in the love of wild places? As you have turned the pages, and moved ever northwards with the unfolding story held in your hands, how do these landscapes speak to you? As you have perchance imagined yourself in many of the locations, what has your emotional response been? Or as you have perhaps recalled a climb or walk that included touching the Watershed in some wild place, have you also called to mind something of the theatre of the landscapes you so enjoyed? As you have become more aware of the wonders of the Watershed, and begun to appreciate more fully its unique qualities, have you been in any

way motivated to don your boots and experience even the smallest part of it for yourself? Within all of these many possibilities, how was your spirit attuned to all that Nature bestowed?

John Muir's verdict:

The seeds of my enduring love of Nature, of the wild places and creatures, were sown during my boyhood in Scotland; all my life's passions grew from that early schooling. So I am in a state of wonder at the discovery and the evidence of this largely continuous artery of wildness running from one end of Scotland to the other; uniting your country, my homeland, by all these wilder landscapes. This is of supreme value – something to be celebrated and cherished; please do not squander it. Take hold of this opportunity; make something of it for Nature and for the human spirit, and for posterity. Create the means to protect it and to ensure that this wellspring of natural goodness can ever flow outwards to replenish and renew.

Note on UNESCO Biosphere Reserves:

Biosphere Reserves incorporate 'core' protected areas for nature conservation with 'buffer' and 'transition' areas – where people live and work – that are managed sustainably. Local stakeholders – such as non-governmental organisations, cultural groups, economic interests, educational institutions, scientists, and local authorities, are involved in the development of the region. This community based approach means both innovative and strongly rooted cultural contexts, traditional ways of life, land use practices, and local knowledge that can often be transferred to other regions.

See MAB pages on UNESCO's website: http://unesco.org

Photography and other key Web-links

Ribbon of Wildness:	www.ribbonofwildness.co.uk
	Friends of the Ribbon of Wildness on [f]
Keith Brame:	www.kbrame.blogspot.com
	www.brame.photoshelter.com
David Lintern:	http://ww.selfpowered.net/
Kerry Muirhead:	http://kerrymuirhead.wix.com/
	kjmphotography
Mike Pennington:	www.geograph.org.uk/profile9715
Richard Kermode:	www.richardkermode.co.uk
Hayley Warriner:	www.pixito.com/hayleyw
Chris Townsend:	www.christownsendoutdoors.com
Colin Meek:	www.watershedrunning.tumbler.com
Norrie Russell:	www.zoominfo.com/p/Norrie-Russel/
John Muir Trust:	www.jmt.org

Environmental Abbreviations

National Nature Reserve	NNR
Site of Special Scientific Interest	SSSI
Special Conservation Area	SAC
Special Protection Area	SPA
National Scenic Area	NSA

Glossary

Bealach	Gaelic name for the pass between two hills, often, but not always a through-route.
Corrie	A steep sided hollow scooped out of the side of a mountain, by glacial action.
Crag or Craig	This usually refers to a steep rough cliff forming the flank of a mountain or hill.
Flow	Terrain that variously includes peat-land, wetlands and blanket bog, mainly but not exclusively in the north of Scotland.
March	A boundary. The Authors sub-division of the Watershed, eg, Northland March.
Scree	Unstable relatively steep slope formed with loose rocks.
Mountains	There are many different forms referred to in this book, including: Fell, Pike, Law, Ben, Beinn, Sgur, Sgurr, Cnoc, Meall, Creag, Sail, and Carn. These denote a variety of meanings such as elevation, character, local derivation, and shape.
Hill names	For a useful guide to the meaning and origin of the names of mountains and hills in Scotland, see: *Scottish Hill Names* by Peter Drummond

Luath Press Limited

committed to publishing well written books worth reading

LUATH PRESS takes its name from Robert Burns, whose little collie Luath (*Gael.,* swift or nimble) tripped up Jean Armour at a wedding and gave him the chance to speak to the woman who was to be his wife and the abiding love of his life. Burns called one of 'The Twa Dogs' Luath after Cuchullin's hunting dog in Ossian's *Fingal*. Luath Press was established in 1981 in the heart of Burns country, and now resides a few steps up the road from Burns' first lodgings on Edinburgh's Royal Mile.

Luath offers you distinctive writing with a hint of unexpected pleasures.

Most bookshops in the UK, the US, Canada, Australia, New Zealand and parts of Europe either carry our books in stock or can order them for you. To order direct from us, please send a £sterling cheque, postal order, international money order or your credit card details (number, address of cardholder and expiry date) to us at the address below. Please add post and packing as follows: UK – £1.00 per delivery address; overseas surface mail – £2.50 per delivery address; overseas airmail – £3.50 for the first book to each delivery address, plus £1.00 for each additional book by airmail to the same address. If your order is a gift, we will happily enclose your card or message at no extra charge.

Luath Press Limited
543/2 Castlehill
The Royal Mile
Edinburgh EH1 2ND
Scotland
Telephone: 0131 225 4326 (24 hours)
Fax: 0131 225 4324
email: sales@luath.co.uk
Website: www.luath.co.uk